D1236432

North Across the River

North Across the River

A CIVIL WAR
TRAIL OF TEARS

RUTH BEAUMONT COOK

CRANE HILL
PUBLISHERS

Special thanks to Jasmine Hodges for her help with this book.

Published by Crane Hill Publishers, www.cranehill.com

Cover design: Bob Weathers
Printed in Canada

Library of Congress Cataloging-in-Publication Data

Cook, Ruth Beaumont.
North across the river: a Civil War trail of tears/Ruth Beaumont Cook.
p.   cm.
Includes bibliographical references and index.
ISBN 1-57587-070-3
1. Atlanta Campaign, 1864—Social aspects. 2. Georgia—History—Civil War, 1861–1865—Refugees. 3. Textile workers—Georgia—Atlanta Region—Relocation—Indiana—History—19th century. 4. Deportation—Georgia—Atlanta Region—History—19th century. 5. United States—History—Civil War, 1861–1865—Refugees. I. Title

E4767.7.C76   1998
973.7'371—dc21   97–49449
                                            CIP

10   9   8   7   6   5   4   3   2   1

For Barney,
who makes all journeys special.

THE TRAIL OF TEARS FOLLOWED BY REFUGEE GEORGIA MILLWORKERS IN 1864.

This map shows the trail of tears traveled by civilian southern cotton mill-workers, which began in Marietta, Georgia, in July 1864, with orders from General William T. Sherman. On duty at a railroad siding, Union Private William Miller watched the refugees pass through Kingston, Georgia, "going north to where they can live until the war is over." Western & Atlantic Railroad cars carried the workers and their families up through Adairsville, Resaca, and Dalton, and then through Ringgold Gap to Union-occupied Chattanooga and Nashville, Tennessee. In Nashville, totally removed from familiar surroundings, they boarded L&N Railroad cars and continued on to Louisville where some remained in refugee prison houses and others crossed the Ohio River in a desperate search for work in Union cotton mills.

TABLE OF CONTENTS

ACKNOWLEDGMENTS

Many people have shared both information and enthusiasm in connection with this project, and I am grateful to every single one of them.

First, to Christine Foster for recognizing a wonderful, mostly untold story and insisting there be time to pursue it. And then to Ellen Sullivan for taking it on and involving me. To Norma McKittrick, my longtime acquaintance and then editor as well as encourager, and to Shelley DeLuca, who brought the manuscript expertly to fruition. To Mary Hanby, my indispensable assistant who loves literature and keeps me organized, and to my writing friends, Marianne Merrill Moates and Elsa Dodd Rutherford, for all of their nudges in the right direction. To my parents and to my sons, Roger and Bob, for their enthusiasm and love. And to my dear husband, Barney, for sharing this and many other journeys in both practical and creative ways.

Thanks to Mary Margaret Bell and Charles Castner with the University Archives and Records Center at University Libraries, University of Louisville (Kentucky); Janie C. Morris and Rod Clare with Rare Book, Manuscript, and Special Collections, Duke University; Vicki Casteel with the Indiana State Archives; Louise Armour DeLong, director, the Archibald Smith Plantation in Roswell, Georgia; Daniel M. Emsweller and his wife, Michele, at the Sweetwater Creek State Park archives center; Sherron D. Lawson with the Roswell Historical Society and Dottie Etris with the Historic Roswell Convention and Visitors Bureau; Bill Jackson, general manager, and staff at the Marietta Conference Center, which stands on the site of the original Georgia Military Institute; and to Skipper Hoke and the Sons of Confederate Veterans, Roswell Mills Camp No. 1547, who plan to dedicate a monument to the Roswell women and children on July 6, 2000.

My thanks also to the library staffs who helped me hunt and gather and gain perspective—especially Yvonne Crumpler and her staff at the Southern History Collection at the Birmingham (Alabama) Public Library; Judy Howe and her staff at the Tell City (Indiana) Public Library; the staff at Cannelton (Indiana) Public Library; Carolyn Davis at the Syracuse University library; Cindy May and the staff at Indiana University's Lilly Library; the staff at the Atlanta History Center; Leigh Darbe at the Indiana Historical Society Library; Bill Cahill and the staff at Sweetwater Creek State Park; Shirley Deuchler and her staff at Bulloch Hall in Roswell; and student intern Jasmine Hodges at Birmingham-Southern College in Birmingham.

I am especially indebted to those individuals whose love of history and storytelling preserved materials that otherwise might have been lost—especially to Michael Hitt of the Roswell Police Department for his painstakingly careful research of both civilian and military events and for the wealth of information he has made available at Bulloch Hall. And to Mike Rutherford and Chuck Poehlein, who have been just as careful in their research and collection at the Old Perry County Courthouse Museum in Cannelton, Indiana. To Gloria Wahl of Historic Cannelton Inc. for sending me initial information and putting me in touch with millworker descendants in Indiana. To James Skinner of Presbyterian College in Clinton, South Carolina, for background information on Roswell, and on Henry Merrell's insights into mill life. And to Monroe King of Douglasville, Georgia, for information and theories about Sweetwater Creek.

This book could never have been written without the wonderful family memories and documents collected by members of the Kendley, Stewart, and Farr families, whose ancestors lived this experience. Many, many thanks to George H. and Elizabeth Kendley of Marietta, Georgia; Mary Ida and Robert Powers of Cannelton, Indiana; Margaret May Schank and her daughter Julie Schank Kunkler of Cannelton; Shirley Sapp of Indianapolis; and Hazel Litherland of Cannelton. Thanks also to Mrs. Hugh Farr and Mrs. David Fairley of Charlotte, North Carolina, and to the family of Synthia Catherine Stewart Boyd, whom I have yet to meet.

INTRODUCTION

A search for "Roswell" on the World Wide Web yields all sorts of information about UFOs and speculation about an alien spaceship crash in Roswell, New Mexico, in 1947. More than eighty years earlier, in the summer of 1864, another (perhaps just as baffling) Roswell incident occurred. It did not involve aliens, but civilian residents of the Confederacy; it totally disrupted their lives and forever changed their relationship to their homes and country.

As we near the end of a century that has witnessed brutal foreign wars, we tend to associate the misery of displaced persons with such faraway lands as Cambodia, Vietnam, Bosnia, Kosovo, and Rwanda. We envision refugees forced from their homes and marching along war-torn highways on other continents, carrying what they can. And yet if we are honest about our own history, we can associate displaced persons with the Cherokee Trail of Tears to Oklahoma in the 1830s and the sand-swept confinements of Japanese-American citizens during World War II.

Most of us, however, are totally unaware that there were also mass deportations of Confederate civilians—many of them women and children—during the American Civil War. This book chronicles two poignant segments of that deportation. It is the story of how, in the summer of 1864, William Tecumseh Sherman created at least three hundred refugees in his own unique way. He ordered the arrest of civilian millworkers in Roswell, Georgia, and charged them with treason for spinning yarn and weaving cloth. Then he shipped them and millworkers from Sweetwater Creek, Georgia, at Union government expense and with army rations, north out of their homeland, up through Tennessee, and on to Louisville, Kentucky. Sherman directed these Confederate refugees to cross the Ohio River and support themselves in Indiana in whatever way they could.

Earlier, when at least four sisters and brothers of the Kendley family decided to take jobs in the Roswell cotton mill because their parents had died and their farming opportunities had evaporated, they did not realize how drastically their decision would affect all of them and all of their descendants. And when Walter Washington Stewart of Sweetwater Creek promised his young wife, Lizzie, that he would come home to defend her and their children if the Yankees ever made it to Atlanta, he had no idea how impossible it would be for him to keep that promise.

Some of these millworkers, completely uprooted from everything they knew, chose to continue the new lives they made for themselves in a totally foreign part of the country. Others put every ounce of energy into returning to their roots, in spite of the fact that little was left for them in the devastated areas near Atlanta where they had once lived.

I compiled this narrative from bits and pieces of tales told about events that took place in Sweetwater Creek and Roswell in the summer of 1864. It traces the life-changing effects of those events and the ways in which memories of them have been handed down through the generations of families from both communities.

For the descendants of many of these millworker families, understanding what actually happened to their great-great-grandparents has taken more than a hundred years and the diligent efforts of more than one family history buff. Other descendants gained additional understanding through interactions with this writer. Perhaps other descendants still do not fully understand the reasons they live where they do and the journey that led earlier members of their families to that place.

People tend to remember only the highlights of what happens to them in dramatic situations, and as time goes on they often embellish those highlights to fit the telling of the tale at any given moment. But within the shell of every adventurous tale nestles at least one grain of truth around which the tale grows and begins to gleam. Even in tales that seem at first glance to be diametrically opposed, plot lines can be traced to the same basic facts.

Wherever possible, I linked the tales of these millworkers and their families to documented information. I made no fabrications about the characters, except where I interwove statements of memory and clearly connected facts to create dramatic scenes.

The detailed information in this book came from conversations with the descendants of the families involved as well as from historic letters and other family memorabilia they shared with me. I look forward to finding out more details as other descendants read this narrative and are prompted to share their family memories.

"Scattered like dust and leaves, when the mighty blasts of October seize them, and whirl them aloft, and sprinkle them far o'er the ocean."

— Henry Wadsworth Longfellow
Evangeline, A Tale of Acadie

PART I
THE STARS
ARE FALLING

CHAPTER 1

FACTORY TOWN ON SWEETWATER CREEK

The memory of one autumn evening in Georgia remained starkly vivid in Synthia Catherine Stewart's mind all her life. She could still recall it clearly eighty-three years later when she made a phonograph record about her life for her grandson way out in Comanche County, Texas.

Synthia Catherine, who was six years old that Georgia evening in 1860, felt her father's hand, callous-thickened from his bossman work at the cotton mill, closing firm and warm around her much smaller one as they hurried down the pathway into Factory Town on the banks of Sweetwater Creek, just west of Atlanta. Only twenty-five years earlier, that pathway had wound through Cherokee land in a dense forest Native Americans had roamed for thousands of years. Back then there was no dam across Sweetwater Creek and no cotton mill next to it.

Synthia Catherine and her father were hurrying to see a show that evening. Walter Washington Stewart would have carried a lantern to light the pine needle–carpeted pathway that absorbed all sound from their footsteps—his long, striding ones and her quicker, double-time ones. The pathway would have been dotted with many lanterns, as it was each morning an hour or so before dawn when the millworkers made their way down that same pathway to be at their jobs when the sun came up.

Perhaps Walter Stewart had promised his daughter this special treat if she did what her mama expected all week. Decades later Synthia Catherine recalled that it seemed as though the residents of the entire company town, all two hundred or so of them, were moving in one purposeful direction that evening—they were going to be entertained.

Four years after that memorable night, Synthia Catherine boarded a Western & Atlantic Railroad car that lurched out of Marietta on its way to a mysterious, mixed-reputation place known simply as "the North." By that time she would well remember the starry autumn evening, but she would not remember the show her father had taken her to see. She would not remember it because the show had been interrupted almost before it began.

"Come out and see! Come out and see!" someone shouted while bursting into the large millroom that served as a meeting hall and at times even a wedding chapel. "The stars are falling! Come out and see!"

Everyone crowded out of the building and down to the sandy, narrow creek bank where they could get a clear view of the night sky. They craned their necks and peered upward. The show in the sky made everyone forget about the show inside the millroom.

"Everybody was watching the stars, and it lasted fifteen or twenty minutes," Synthia Catherine told her grandson. The meteor shower was impressive, with four and five stars streaking at a time. "They didn't fall, they just streaked over the sky," recalled Synthia Catherine.

People living in 1860 understood that meteors, small and solid other-worldly bodies, could enter the earth's atmosphere and be transformed by friction into fiery shooting stars. Lewis Collins's *History of Kentucky* recorded a shower of shooting stars, which he also referred to as "small meteors," on November 13, 1834. He said the shower lasted from eleven o'clock on a Tuesday night until broad daylight the next morning. Many stars fell directly to the earth, and others came down at a slant or "shot in a parallel direction until their explosion without noise," wrote Collins. Some created long streaks of light like needles, and some looked like "a storm of fire" or snowflakes. Collins declared the whole display "grand, sublime, and terrible."

The millworkers in Sweetwater Creek probably did not know much about astronomy. But whether or not they understood that shooting stars were meteors, they still considered them a sign from the heavens, a sign like the Wise Men's star in the Bible. And so a woman in the crowd on the creek bank that evening asked an age-old question, a question people craning their necks toward night skies had asked for centuries: "What does it mean, do you suppose?"

It was Synthia Catherine's father who stepped forward to answer the woman's question. As a bossman he was somewhat of an authority figure in Factory Town. He told the men, women, and children standing on the creek bank that the shooting stars predicted war. As Synthia Catherine explained to her grandson many years later when she made the phonograph record, her father said "the North was going to cause war against the South on account of the Negroes. They were going to free the Negroes, get them away from the South because they did so much work, made so much cotton, and made lots of money, and they [the Northerners] wanted to break this all up."

Factory Town, which was also called Factory Shoals, was not built into the high ridges along Sweetwater Creek until the late 1840s, and Walter Stewart did not come to this place from his father's farm in Forsyth County until 1851. Beforehand the whole area belonged to the Cherokee, but their reluctant departure left room for a whole new way of life to take root in north and west Georgia—the gold mines, farms, and mills of American settlers.

The Brevard Fault zone runs along the basin of Sweetwater Creek, where the shifting of one giant slab of the earth's crust against another slab made the land surrounding this creek more mountainous than that surrounding other creeks in this part of Georgia. High cliffs studded with oak, poplar, and beech trees line the banks of Sweetwater Creek.

Legend says that "Sweetwater" translates the name of Chief Ama-Kanasta and that the steep "Jack's Hills" on the south side of

Sweetwater Creek are named for Chief Jack, who is rumored to be buried nearby. Even though the Cherokee were evicted long ago, the ridges high above the creek still echo with the melodious names they bestowed, including Chattanooga, the "pointed rock," and Dahlonega, the "yellow" gold.

The Cherokee, more than any other Native American population, revised their culture in keeping with American ideas, yet no tribal senate or house of representatives, no constitution, alphabet, or tribal public school system could endear them to the American settlers in Georgia. Advancements in Cherokee culture only heightened the settlers' distrust. No matter what the Cherokee did, the settlers still considered them to be too "Indian," a word automatically associated with "savage." And the Cherokee were never great American allies. Again and again they had sided with the British—before and during the Revolutionary War and again during the War of 1812.

But it was gold greed as much as land greed that sealed the fate of the Cherokee nation in Georgia. As early as 1819, when the precious metal first attracted attention on tribal lands, the State of Georgia appealed to the United States government to remove the Cherokee. Georgia failed in that attempt, but state officials kept pushing for the removal of the Cherokee and eventually gained a powerful ally in Andrew Jackson.

When America's first major gold rush erupted near Dahlonega, the Cherokee appealed to the federal government for protection because the Georgia legislature had outlawed their government and confiscated their lands. Andrew Jackson, who had just been elected president for the first of two terms, defied the U.S. Supreme Court and rejected the appeal.

It was not until 1838 that federal troops began forcibly evicting the Cherokee from Georgia and Alabama. A few hundred members of the tribe escaped to the mountains of North Carolina, where they purchased land and incorporated, but nearly twenty thousand others were driven west to Oklahoma via the Trail of Tears. Almost four thousand of those refugees lost their lives to hunger, disease, and exposure while traveling that three hundred–mile trail. The last members of the Cherokee nation officially left Georgia by the end of 1838; the state government already had begun to divide the tribe's land through lotteries, even as early as 1827.

At the end of 1831, Georgia's General Assembly ordered all Cherokee land surveyed and distributed by lottery. This was done in spite of the U.S. Supreme Court's decree that Georgia had no authority to outlaw the Cherokee government.

Phillip J. Crask was eager to win a forty-acre gold lot in the series of lotteries held in 1832. Since Crask lived in Baldwin County, it is likely he traveled to Milledgeville, the state capital, to watch the lottery drawings. On pre-announced days, state officials turned two large wheels—one stuffed with the names of would-be winners and the other stuffed with the numbers of would-be land prizes. The officials published the "matches" in the *Gold and Land Lottery Register,* which people could buy at their county courthouse for five dollars a copy if they couldn't travel to Milledgeville to attend the lottery drawings.

Crask qualified for the lottery because he was at least eighteen years old and had lived in Georgia for more than three years. He might even have been standing in the crowd in Milledgeville when his name was called and he was matched with Lot 929 in District 18 of the Second Section.

Lot 929, which was where the Sweetwater Creek mill would begin operation in 1849, was just eleven miles east of Villa Rica, where gold had already been discovered. We do not know exactly when Crask shouldered his pack and headed out to prospect for his fortune, but we do know that many of his fellow lottery winners waited until after state officials and the Cherokee met at New Echota and signed a treaty in December 1835. According to the treaty a group of Cherokee leaders agreed to cede tribal territory in the eastern United States in exchange for almost six million dollars plus a tract of land in Indian territory that later became part of the state of Oklahoma. More than nine-tenths of the tribe denounced this transaction, but it took place anyway, making western Georgia slightly more "safe" for American settlers and prospectors, who were often referred to as "those forty-acre people."

Apparently Crask's vision of riches evaporated rather quickly once he began prospecting along the banks of Sweetwater Creek. Gilded nuggets never appeared in the bottom of his circular panning dish, and he probably did not see any other value to the land prize for which he had paid an $18 grant fee. By 1837, five years after the Georgia Gold Lottery, Crask had failed to pay any taxes, so his land was sold at an auction held on the courthouse steps to John Boyle for $12.50. Boyle held the land for eight years, then turned a handsome profit in 1845, when he sold it for $500 to Charles J. McDonald of Cobb County, a former governor of Georgia, and his business partner, Colonel James Rogers of Milledgeville.

Rogers and McDonald recognized immediately that the lay of their new land along Sweetwater Creek was ideal for a water-powered factory. By November 1846 the *Milledgeville Southern Recorder* was reporting that "another factory is now in progress of erection near the line of this county and Campbell by Messers McDonald and Rogers. It is thought that it will be in full operation some time during the ensuing year." That prediction proved to be slightly ambitious. The mill finally went into full production on December 21, 1849.

Sweetwater Creek has often been called "the flat shoals," and for good reason. The great upended slabs of rock that line the creek bed and banks are not rounded at all—they look like petrified slices of wet, charcoal-gray tree trunk. These flat shoals offer a twenty-three-foot fall of water that in 1849 could be harnessed to power machinery. And the addition of a manmade, rock-lined millrace could enhance the water power by diverting the rushing creek to the mill wheel at an even faster pace.

The flat shoals of Sweetwater Creek offered a twenty-three-foot fall of water, enhanced by a manmade, rock-lined millrace to divert rushing creek water to the mill wheel. *(Photo by Barney Cook)*

Today, visitors hiking along the edge of the creek on a mellow autumn Saturday can easily imagine the bustle of construction in that dense stretch of woods between 1846 and 1849. Lumbermen tagged trees, brought them crashing down, then dragged them off to a local sawmill to plane them out for support beams and scaffoldings. Other laborers scoured downstream to quarry the flat gray stones that were fitted in place for the millrace and the mill foundations. Still others fired red bricks right on the mill property for the four upper stories.

Up through the thick stand of trees rose a five-story building just at the edge of the creek. Even today, peeking through the chain-link fence that surrounds these now silent and still-charred ruins, visitors can follow the form of the structure—its massive two-foot-thick walls and its limestone-bordered window openings that fanned inward to allow as much light as possible into each workroom. Ever fearful of fire catching the flammable cotton lint, mill officials rarely allowed open-flame light sources inside the building.

Today in autumn the faded rose and yellow tints of the bricks blend wistfully with similar hues in the trees on the opposite creek bank. The skeletal remains of the upper stories still retain the dark charring from the fires deliberately set more than one hundred thirty years ago.

Even while the mill was being built, Charles McDonald was already deeply concerned about whether Georgia would find it necessary to secede from the Union. One day, as he and a Marietta newspaper editor rode horseback near the construction site, McDonald speculated about the growing possibility of a Southern confederacy. "Many of the most prominent men in the Southern states have already pledged their support," he told the editor. "They see it as a reality, and they have already decided upon Atlanta as the capital."

Charles McDonald and James Rogers incorporated their enterprise as Sweetwater Manufacturing Company, patterned after the cotton mills already in operation in Roswell, on another tributary of the Chattahoochee River farther north. They equipped their building with state-of-the-art machinery, including a great beast of a waterwheel that weighed more than forty thousand pounds. A complex series of shafts, gears, and leather belts connected each individual loom and spinning machine to every other machine in the building. The water in the millrace turned the mighty wheel, which turned the single driveshaft. As the teeth of the gears meshed, movement spread out to all the looms and spinners.

According to its owners, Sweetwater Manufacturing Company was in business to "manufacture, bleach, dye, print, and finish all goods of which cotton or other fibrous materials form a part, and to manufacturer [sic] flour from wheat or grain of any kind, and all machinery used for such purposes or any other, and to erect such mills and other works as may be necessary to carry on their business."

In 1851, two years after the cotton mill portion of Sweetwater Manufacturing Company began operation, Walter Washington Stewart brought his fifteen-year-old wife, Charlotte Elizabeth (Lizzie) Russell Stewart, to Factory Town. The couple's descendants say that Walter, age twenty-two at the time, worked as a "bossman in the mill," and historians at Sweetwater Creek say his first house stood on a ridge above the creek gorge.

Walter and Lizzie Stewart began raising a family almost immediately. Sarah E. was born in 1852, followed by Synthia Catherine in 1854, James Buchanan in 1857, and Linnie Isabella in 1859.

Lizzie carried cool, clear drinking water from the community spring, and the Stewarts shopped at the company store. In typical milltown fashion, they could purchase all the necessities of life, as well as a few luxuries such as books and ribbons, on credit. For anything else they relied on the teamsters who drove the cotton mill wagons to Marietta and Atlanta several times a week.

The main "street" of the town, Sweetwater Factory Road, ran parallel to the creek and then on to Ferguson's Crossing, a half mile north. The road continued across the bridge at Ferguson's Crossing, the last bridge over the creek before it emptied into the Chattahoochee River, and then on to the railhead in Atlanta.

In 1860 the Sweetwater Manufacturing Company store stood beside Sweetwater Factory Road, but all that is visible today is an excavated, leaf-filled depression at the base of a tree-studded hillside. The building rose three stories high, which probably made it second to the mill as the tallest building in the vicinity. Millworkers and their families shopped for food, hardware, clothing, and sundries on the first floor. The second floor served as a storage area, and the third floor provided living quarters for either the store's proprietor or one of the mill superintendents.

The mill managers built a few houses high on the wooded ridge above the factory buildings and rented them to families such as the Demooneys and the Humphries. Many other workers lived on farms in the surrounding countryside. A. J. and Margaret White may have lived in one of the rented houses with their two small children. Several families of Tutchstones and Causeys reportedly worked in the mill and lived nearby.

Working in the cotton mill offered both advantages and disadvantages compared to other means of earning a living. Adults earned more per hour than they might have made in the past for farm labor or weaving and sewing at home, and they could work more regular hours. The newer machinery available in the 1850s and 1860s relied less on human muscle power, so many of the spindles and looms and carding tools could be operated by women and children. Since there were no child labor laws at the time, ten-year-old boys and girls often worked right along with their parents while grandmothers tended the younger children at home.

Even the children had to obey strict rules about arriving on time and not slacking off during working hours. One slip and the family paycheck might show a deduction. Millworkers put in long hours, and the bossmen were always pushing to speed up production.

The air inside a mill like the one at Sweetwater Creek was always heavy with lint from the cotton, lint that clung to the clothes and hair of the workers. The parents who worked at the Sweetwater Creek mill taught their children to breathe through their noses whenever they were inside the building to try to keep the lint from sneaking into their lungs. In the 1800s people feared consumption. They did not know what caused it, but they knew it could make a death march through any person with weak lungs.

The Sweetwater Creek mill was a busy place, taking in huge bales of cotton delivered in groups of four by mule and supply wagon from Atlanta and Marietta. The mules pulled up to an entrance that opened onto an upper floor, because the process of creating yarn worked its way down from the top of the building to the bottom. When Walter Stewart first worked at the mill, it buzzed with the noise of six thousand spindles and ninety looms and produced seven hundred fifty pounds of yarn each day.

Three years before the beginning of the Civil War, Charles McDonald reorganized the Sweetwater Manufacturing Company as New Manchester Manufacturing Company, naming it after Manchester, England, the center of the British textile industry. James Rogers apparently had left the company before this time because his name is not mentioned in the 1857 transaction.

The window openings of the mill on Sweetwater Creek fanned inward to allow as much light as possible into each workroom. Cotton bales were delivered in groups of four by mule and supply wagon from Atlanta and Marietta. The entrance was on an upper floor because the process of creating yarn worked its way from the top floor to the bottom. *(Photo by Barney Cook)*

McDonald sold his personal interest to the new corporation for the sum of fifty thousand dollars. This expenditure apparently did not deplete the funds of the corporation because new machinery was added to the mill at this time. The mill output soon tripled.

Officially, Factory Town became New Manchester, as marked on the maps in Campbell County (later Douglas County), Georgia. The town had a population of approximately two hundred and its own post office, most likely located inside the company store.

By 1860 the workers in the New Manchester Manufacturing Company cotton mill were taking in seven hundred pounds of cotton per day and transforming the fluffy fibers into one hundred twenty bunches of yarn and five hundred yards of osnaburg, a fabric that was popular with the textile industry in the 1800s. Originally the term referred to a coarse linen cloth made in Germany, but by 1860 it had become the name of a strong, unbleached cotton fabric that was loosely woven and lighter than canvas but heavier than linen. Osnaburg was used as an inexpensive dress fabric as well as a material for making sacking and tents.

On that fall evening in 1860, when Synthia Catherine Stewart and her father, Walter, watched the meteor shower from the banks of Sweetwater Creek, the five-story mill building they had just left stood taller than any building in bustling Atlanta, which was just twenty-five miles away. Not long after that evening, Walter quit his job as bossman at the mill. He could clearly see the storm clouds gathering on the horizon of national unity, and he apparently assumed—quite correctly—that enlistment in a rebel army could not be far off for him.

Abraham Lincoln was elected president in November, and South Carolina defiantly adopted its Ordinance of Secession on December 20. Sometime during 1861 Walter Stewart took the ambitious step of purchasing a farm not far from the mill. He wanted more security for his family if he had to go and fight. He

Charles J. McDonald and Colonel James Rogers erected a water-powered cotton mill on the banks of Sweetwater Creek in Campbell County (now Douglas County), Georgia, between 1846 and 1849. *(Photo by Barney Cook)*

built a house on the farm and had in mind that if the need arose, his wife, Lizzie, could work in the cotton mill while maintaining the farm as security.

Between January and May 1861, a parade of ten Southern states followed South Carolina out of the Union. Jefferson Davis agreed in February to become their leader, and the fateful shots of Fort Sumter were fired in Charleston Harbor on April 12. It was General Pierre Gustave Toutant Beauregard who ordered those first shots fired. After thirty-four hours of incessant shelling, it was with a sad sort of irony that General Beauregard accepted the surrender of the small Fort Sumter garrison from Major Robert Anderson, his former instructor and ally at the United States Military Academy at West Point.

Walter Stewart most likely shook his head and frowned when he heard reports of these events and their negative effect on camaraderie. Yes, he told Synthia Catherine, it was all happening just as he had thought it would. The North was most certainly about to cause war on the South.

When Synthia Catherine's second little brother was born on September 4, Walter and Lizzie patriotically named him Jefferson Davis Stewart. Walter enlisted in the Army of the Confederacy on March 4, 1862, as a member of Company K, Forty-first Regiment, Georgia Volunteer Infantry, Army of Tennessee, a unit known as the Campbell Salt Springs Guards. At least two other New Manchester residents joined the Campbell Salt Springs Guards when Walter Stewart did: John Benjamin Humphries, age nineteen, and William J. Newbern, age twenty-three.

Just as he correctly predicted war in the fall of 1860, Walter Stewart obviously foresaw his departure from New Manchester for military service. Perhaps he even envisioned the Northern imprisonment he would later experience.

Although Walter Stewart made provisions for the financial threats his wife and family might endure, it is doubtful he anticipated the uprooting they would experience after he marched away— an uprooting not unlike what the Cherokee endured a quarter century earlier. And though Lizzie Stewart most certainly feared for her husband's life and for the safety of their growing family, it is doubtful she had any inkling of the tearful trail that she and most of her children would soon be forced to follow.

CHAPTER 2

MILL VILLAGE AT ROSWELL

The story of this Civil War trail of tears cannot be fully told without first describing the beginnings of another mill village a number of years earlier at Roswell, just outside Atlanta. It is also necessary to describe the background of several brothers and sisters named Kendley, who, like the Stewarts of Sweetwater Creek, lived out a destiny they could not have imagined before 1864.

The first cotton mill in Roswell, Georgia, was built more than ten years before the cotton mill in Sweetwater Creek. It, too, was connected to the state-run gold and land lotteries. When Benjamin Parks overturned a gold-laced rock in north Georgia in 1828, his discovery lured dreamers from everywhere and quickly launched the boomtowns of Auraria and Dahlonega. The Bank of Darien, down on the eastern sea island coast of the state, decided to send Roswell King Sr. up to these new boom-towns to establish a branch and bring a degree of order to a chaotic financial situation. Before King arrived the gold miners had to rely on the bank of the Pigeon Roost Mining Company and the Farmers Bank of Chattahoochy (the actual spelling of the bank name) to protect their deposits from outlaws.

Before he was sent to north Georgia, Roswell King and his son, who was his namesake, managed two south Georgia plantations for absentee Philadelphia owner Pierce Butler. The King family left Connecticut in the 1700s and also established successful rice, cotton, and lumber businesses in Darien.

Roswell King Sr. rode to the north Georgia gold country as a representative of the Bank of Darien when he was in his early sixties. On horseback, King followed Indian trails northwest from Savannah. He passed into Cherokee territory north of where Vickery's

Roswell King Sr. established the Roswell Manufacturing Company in 1839 and built his first cotton mill on the banks of Vickery's Creek in what became Roswell (Cobb County), Georgia. *(Photo by Barney Cook of a painting by Ernest DeVane that hangs in the council chambers at City Hall in Roswell, Georgia.)*

Creek continues to flow into the Chattahoochee River in the modern-day Atlanta suburb that bears his first name.

The stream was called Cedar Creek when Roswell King first rode alongside it during his trip in the early 1830s. Some legends say the creek's final name, Vickery's, came from a Cherokee woman who lived near its headwaters and operated a ferry across the Chattahoochee. Perhaps King met Sharlot Vickery and led his horse onto her ferry to cross the river. And perhaps it was King who continued the association of her name with the creek, even though she was forced to leave the area when the Cherokee were driven out in the late 1830s.

On this trip King passed through the lands of the Chattahoochee and continued on to Auraria. The place was bursting with prospectors, tradesmen, and settlers. Auraria's population was approaching ten thousand, and each resident dreamed of riches in gold, land, or some offshoot business. King had different visions, although some say he also was interested in gold and invested in the mines. One description of him mentions blue powder marks on his face when he was injured in a gold mine explosion.

Roswell King's dream was to backtrack his route to the Chattahoochee tributaries and carve out an upcountry retreat in the wilderness. He wanted to bring his wealthy south Georgia planter friends to a place where they could escape the sultry heat and malaria-ridden vapors of Darien, Savannah, Midway, and Sunbury. Like most people of the 1800s, King regarded fresh air as a key component of good health. He considered the upland climate of north Georgia ideal.

One person who has researched Roswell King in recent years thinks he had other reasons for settling in north Georgia. Michael Hitt, a Roswell police officer, believes there was more to Roswell King's decision than just climate preference. "He decided to move north permanently," says Hitt. "First and foremost, Roswell King was a cut-and-dried businessman. There had to be a good reason for him to leave behind his successful businesses around Darien and move himself and his friends to the middle of the wilderness." Hitt thinks the financial panic of inflated land values and the wild-cat banking that culminated in an economic depression in 1837 had something to do with King's move.

Whatever his true motives were, Roswell King wanted to harness the power of Vickery's Creek. Just as Charles McDonald and James Rogers would do ten years later at Sweetwater Creek, King envisioned huge waterwheels and endless linkages of shafts and gears and leather belts to transform cotton into yarn and fabric.

King probably knew about steam engines and the fact that one had been used to power a cotton mill in England fifty years earlier.

But steam was not yet a practical fuel in Georgia in the 1830s; it would not power a cotton mill in the United States until 1847. Besides, steam engines did not like wood as a fuel—they had huge appetites for coal. It would have cost a small fortune to bring enough coal to this part of Georgia to power anything—and the water of Vickery's Creek was there waiting to be harnessed.

Roswell King began acquiring title to hundreds of acres of land in the vicinity of the Chattahoochee River. Although he purchased most of his holdings through agents and speculators, he entered the 1832 gold lottery on his own behalf. When state officials drew the tickets, King became the fortunate holder of Lot 454 in District 15 of Section 2, a tract located in what first became Cobb County and later Fulton County, where King established his combination cotton planter retreat and milltown. King's land was three districts north and one district east of the Sweetwater Creek land that Phillip J. Crask won in the same lottery.

Between 1834 and 1836, King began building his cotton mill— an earth- and rock-filled dam and a wooden millrace with a stone foundation. He supervised a small group of workers, possibly slaves he brought with him from the coast or disillusioned miners from the gold-rush boomtowns, who worked for him with simple tools and bare hands.

First King's workers hiked upstream and created temporary cofferdams by hollowing out logs and filling them with rocks. They placed these rock-filled logs to "unwater" a section of Vickery's Creek by diverting it into a sluice. Once this section was dry, the workers began the slow process of creating the dam. Teams of laborers dragged massive hardwood timbers into the muck of the creekbed. Layer upon layer, they piled the timbers until they reached thirty feet high. Then the workers would drag rock, debris, and earth to carefully compress it all into a watertight concoction.

King and his laborers knew that, once allowed back into its natural banks, Vickery's Creek would push hour after hour and day after day to undermine this watertight concoction. As long as the waters failed to break through, the creek would redirect its force into the millrace and create the power to drive spindles and looms in a mill constructed just below the dam.

While the millrace and dam were under construction, King built a log cabin with glass windows and pine floors. By 1838 he had cast his personal lot with his new colony and what would become Roswell Manufacturing Company. At the time, only ten or twelve other textile mills existed in all of Georgia, and all of them were small.

The original cotton mill building in Roswell began to go up in late 1838. Like Sweetwater Creek, where construction would begin seven years later, the brick upper floors rose up through the trees along Vickery's Creek from a stone foundation. Designed like most mills of that time, the top floor—in this case the third

A portion of one fading redbrick wall of the original Roswell cotton mill is still visible today from a rock-walled pathway that winds down a heavily wooded hillside. *(Photo by Barney Cook)*

This massive gear mechanism lies silent on a hillside now, but it was feeding power to a full-capacity cotton mill when Colonel Abram O. Miller led a detail of the Seventy-second Indiana Mounted Infantry into Roswell on July 6, 1864. *(Photo by Barney Cook)*

floor—housed the carding and picking operations, the first steps in producing cotton yarn and fabric. The third floor of the Roswell mill building also had an attic that would eventually hold mules— spinning machines that female workers could use to produce thread from cotton fiber. This machinery was added after the mill began operation.

The second floor of the Roswell mill housed the spinning room. The first floor was designed for weaving, but the weaving machinery was installed after the mill opened.

The basement, which was closed, contained no machinery other than the driving drum.

At three stories high with a base of forty-eight by eighty-eight feet, the first Roswell cotton mill was considerably smaller than the Sweetwater Creek mill would be, but during the years before the Civil War, the Roswell mill spawned a much larger and more permanent community than Sweetwater Creek did. Although the Roswell community survived, only a very small remnant of the original Roswell mill remains. Visitors who venture down the heavily wooded, rock-walled pathway to its site will see a portion of a fading redbrick wall and massive rusted metal ductwork and gears. Those pieces remain, thanks to the efforts of various Roswell Historical Society members, archaeologists, and researchers who braved steep slopes, stubborn kudzu vines, and erroneous theories to chart carefully the mill's exact location and provide explanations about it.

One of those researchers is James L. Skinner, an English professor at Presbyterian College in South Carolina. When Skinner's family inherited the Archibald Smith property in Roswell, he discovered the memoir of Henry Merrell, who served as an assistant agent in the mill's early days, tucked away in a drawer in the home.

Henry Merrell was in Lexington, Kentucky, in 1838 when a friend told him that several Georgia planter families were establishing a manufacturing community in Georgia's recently opened Cherokee territory. Merrell wrote to Roswell King's son Barrington and offered to help set up and run the new mill. Barrington accepted his offer.

The twenty-three-year-old Merrell, who was trained at the Oneida mills near Utica, New York, arrived in Roswell with machinery that was shipped from Paterson, New Jersey. Merrell had weak lungs and ventured south partly because he thought the climate would be better for his health. He recorded his thoughts and impressions in a diary, from which Skinner has produced *The Autobiography of Henry Merrell*. In a sense, Merrell serves as a bridge of understanding about the relationship between traditional southern gentry and the millworkers they hired to produce profits for them through the manufacture of yarn and fabric.

The Roswell Manufacturing Company was established in 1839. Its incorporators were Roswell King Sr., his sons Barrington and Ralph, John Dunwody, James S. Bulloch, Henry Atwood, and the heirs of Bayard E. Hand, who were Roswell King's grandchildren. Bayard Hand, his daughter Eliza's husband, died in Darien about the time the mill was being constructed. King urged Eliza to travel north and raise her three small children in his household in Roswell.

During the winter of 1839, Roswell King pulled laborers away from mill construction to complete a comfortable home for himself, his daughter, and her family. Primrose Cottage, just northeast of the town square on what is now Mimosa Boulevard, became the first permanent home in Roswell. King's wife, Catherine, and many other members of his family remained in Darien during the construction period. Catherine died in Darien that year, without ever seeing the colony, the cottage, or the mill her husband developed.

Wealthy planters of southern coastal Georgia soon followed, responding enthusiastically to Roswell King's invitation to establish a colony at Roswell. First came his son Barrington, who traveled three hundred miles in a wagon from the sea coast with his wife, nine children, a tutor, and the family servants.

Major James Stephens Bulloch and his brother-in-law, John Dunwody, brought their families from the Savannah area. Roswell police officer and researcher Michael Hitt believes that the Bulloch and Dunwody families first occupied cabins built by Cherokee who left the area in 1836.

Hitt also believes that Bulloch and Dunwody, like Roswell King, came to north Georgia for reasons other than climate. Bulloch was president of the United States Bank's branch office in Savannah, a branch Hitt and other sources suggest was under investigation because of mismanagement. When the national bank panic occurred in 1837, many lost fortunes held by United States Bank branches.

Archibald Smith brought his family from St. Mary's and established a farm about a mile north of the Roswell town square. The Smiths cultivated grass fields and cotton in spite of problems with dewberries and broomstraw.

King offered these people and others who moved north the opportunity to purchase stock in the new Roswell Manufacturing Company, and many did so. They came to help settle the new north

Georgia town and, in several years' time, built stately homes that echoed the Greek Revival mansions of south Georgia. King laid out his colony in the manner of many New England milltowns. It had a fashionable residential district where mansions stood to the west of a town square. To the east were business and worker residential areas, often referred to as "mill village."

A church was one of the first buildings completed, as was done in all good southern towns. Most of the early Roswell landowners were Presbyterians, and they quickly invited Dr. Nathaniel Pratt of the Darien Presbyterian Church to travel north and become their pastor. In October 1839 fifteen of the early "colonists" met with Dr. Pratt in the parlor of King's Primrose Cottage to organize. King donated the land for the Roswell Presbyterian Church, where Dr. Pratt preached his first sermon in May 1840. King later donated land on the west side of town for the Methodist church, which the Kendley family and most millworkers attended.

When it came to "urban planning," King proved himself to be a forward thinker for his time. Not only did he construct company houses for supervisors and bossmen, but he also built apartment buildings for general workers. Apartment buildings were highly unusual in Georgia, and the ones King built may have been the only ones in the South at that time. Constructed of sturdy brick, the buildings on Sloan Street in mill village provided apartments for many of the people who worked in the Roswell cotton mill. Each apartment had a kitchen-living room on the ground floor; bedrooms on the second floor at the top of a steep, narrow stairway; and fireplaces with crude mantels fashioned of heart pine.

Today, two of these buildings house private offices and a dining club. However, it is not difficult to imagine fourteen-year-old factory hand Nancy Fretwell stirring the contents of a cooking pot over a fire while her sisters sat with their mother, Lavina, at a trestle table in one of the apartments. In 1860, Atlanta Lindsey might have been right next-door, stirring her cooking pot while her three young factory-hand daughters, Phebe, Amanda, and Elizabeth, marched the younger Lindsey children up the narrow staircase to pallets on a bedroom floor. The Kendley children, five sisters and three brothers, might have lived here too as they struggled to make ends meet after their parents died.

Millworkers earned eight dollars a month in the 1840s. They bought their own food and clothing, but the cost of living was low. They could buy bacon for four cents a pound, chickens for five cents each, and eggs for five cents a dozen.

When the Roswell cotton mill first began operation, the company store stood alongside the winding road that led from town to the mill. A miller's house and a boardinghouse also stood alongside the road. When the store outgrew its quarters, the company built a new one fifty yards farther up the hill toward town.

In the 1840s Henry Merrell wrote that "one had to be considerable of a goat to get about" the mill business in Roswell. He described wearing out his shoes every week or two, overseeing the cotton mill from lower room to upper room, then climbing up the road to the company store, then walking from there to the cotton gin, and then over to the woolen factory.

When Henry Merrell arrived in Roswell in 1839, he found the town still "in the bushes and very stumpy," with a cow path for what would become Atlanta Street. After attending an Independence Day dinner at Roswell King's home on July 4, he wrote that the stumps and bushes explained why the refined ladies of Roswell scratched themselves so much in spite of their otherwise impeccable manners; the leaves of the underbrush around town were swarming with "red bug," a southern insect with a very itchy bite.

Merrell was surprised at the elaborate manners of the Roswell landowners and their habit of shaking hands and chatting with each other each time they met. Coming from the busy North, he was not accustomed to such behavior.

Soon after Merrell's arrival, Barrington King showed him the foundation of the cotton mill, which Roswell King had completed before Barrington's arrival. The foundation walls were cracking and giving way under the weight of the three brick stories above. Barrington King and Merrell agreed to take the risk of shoring up the building and replacing the defective parts of the old foundation with hewn granite. This required time but worked successfully.

Merrell supervised the installation of the cotton mill's machinery and handled the daily operations of both the mill and the company store. He purchased one share of Roswell Manufacturing Company stock for seven hundred fifty dollars and played an active role in stockholder meetings.

By 1841 Merrell had the original cotton mill in full operation, and people throughout town heard its machinery droning even though they could not see the building from the streets. They also heard the factory bell tolling the hours to begin and end work. When Barrington King stood in the middle of the town square and looked in the direction of the mill, he saw only thick stands of hardwood trees stretching down both sides of the creek. The frenzy of mill activity occurred in a gorge reached by steep, winding dirt roads lined with rock walls built by his father's slaves. Most of the houses of the landowners and the millworkers stood on level land above the creek gorge.

In 1841 the Roswell cotton mill employed only twenty-eight hands, who operated twenty-eight spindles. The workers made their way to the mill each morning at sunrise and heard the rushing water growing louder and louder as they walked down toward the mill building beside Vickery's Creek. Once the warning bell sounded and the engines churned into action, the workers—the general factory hands, machinists, carders, reelers, and weavers—heard the constant rushing of the water mixed with the creaks and roars of the machinery reverberating throughout the workrooms.

The millworkers followed their eleven-hour work schedule six days a week and rested only on the Sabbath. In keeping with their employers' temperance rules, millworkers did not bring alcohol anywhere near the factory. In keeping with the keen fear of fire because of the pervasive lint in the air, they also did not bring matches or any other means of producing a flame inside the building or onto the grounds.

In many respects, Merrell was the first "middle class" person to live in Roswell. He did not have the high social status of the landed gentry like the planter families, yet he enjoyed higher social standing than the skilled and unskilled workers he supervised at the mill. Merrell considered himself an equal of the planters in birth, education, and refinement, but took pains to point out that northern young men were expected to train for a career "in case of future reverses of fortune" whether they ever planned to actually work or not.

Merrell sometimes took great pride in taking off his coat, rolling up his sleeves, and performing sweat-producing work alongside his weavers and spinners in the mill. After he married Archibald Smith's sister-in-law, Elizabeth Pye Magill, in 1841, the planter families frowned upon him for working with his hands. Even though this did not bother Merrell, he took care not to offend his wife's sensibilities by making an issue of it. He seemed almost to have set himself a mission to defend the dignity of labor in Roswell.

At one point, Merrell thought he found a willing disciple for his work ethic in Barrington King's oldest son, Charles. For several years the boy came and worked with Merrell in the mill every day after school. Merrell saw he had a natural aptitude for mechanics in addition to his "gentlemanly ways." But Charles went away to college and studied to become a Presbyterian minister.

Merrell did not fail completely, however, in passing along his work ethic. James Roswell King and Thomas Edward King, also Barrington's sons, established Ivy Woolen Mill in the 1840s and were very involved in its management. James Roswell King studied manufacturing in Paterson, New Jersey, while Thomas Edward King learned to handle the business side of the operation. Even Barrington Jr. went north to learn shipbuilding before the Civil War, and a number of Dr. Pratt's sons also became involved in manufacturing.

In his diary Merrell hinted that millworkers in Roswell were more difficult to organize and discipline than those he supervised in New York. He referred to the Georgia workers as a "rough population I had to deal with" and as "my wild Arab hands." Part of the difficulty may have been that few, if any, Georgians were used to the regimen of factory labor. In one diary entry, Merrell notes that many of the millworkers were disillusioned gold miners and "forty-acre people" whose only asset was the value of their lottery land. They had little education, no experience in owning substantial assets, and little vision of a progressive future for themselves or their families.

Roswell King died in 1844 at the age of seventy-eight, living long enough to see his milltown and its wealthy landowner colony well established. His family laid him to rest among the stately oaks of the Presbyterian cemetery on a knoll above Vickery's Creek near his cotton mill. King's grave, with its tall obelisk, lies in what is now called Founders' Cemetery on Sloan Street in Roswell. His epitaph reads: "He was the founder of the village which bears his name. A man of great energy, industry, and perseverance, of rigid integrity, truth, and justice, he early earned and long enjoyed the esteem and confidence of his fellow men."

Barrington King was forty-six when he succeeded his father as president of Roswell Manufacturing Company and expanded the mill beyond his father's modest efforts. He enlarged the original mill by adding additional fly spindles and eight more frames so it could produce six hundred fifty pounds of No. 16 yarn and four hundred pounds of cotton rope per day. Barrington also built a second, larger mill building a mile and a half upstream. This new factory had an overshot iron waterwheel and enough contemporary machinery to produce twenty-five hundred pounds of No. 20 yarn each day.

Merrell left Roswell in 1845 for Greene County, Georgia, where he established another cotton mill at Long Shoals on the Oconee River. He remained there until 1856, when he moved to Arkansas.

By 1849, men, women, and children were operating thirty-five hundred spindles and forty looms in the Roswell cotton mill. More than one hundred fifty "lintheads," as they were often called, tended the machines that coiled thousands of bundles of yarn and wove thousands of yards of shirting and osnaburg each week. For their work, employees such as James Dodgen and Pinkney Fields earned one dollar and fifty cents per week, payable in company scrip that was redeemable only at the Roswell Manufacturing Company store.

Jonathan Farr came to Roswell in 1849 and took a job in one of the cotton mills. He brought his wife, Jane Elizabeth Alexander Farr, and his young son, Samuel. Workers like Farr paid rent for their housing, either in the many company houses or in the apartments that have come to be called "The Old Bricks." Rent was deducted before the millworkers received their company scrip pay.

In about 1853 Barrington King added a four-story brick machine shop on the banks of Vickery's Creek. Except for its foundation, which is now partially buried in a massive blanket of kudzu vines, the machine shop remains visible below the restored mill buildings built later just off Mill Street in Roswell.

Barrington King, son of the founder of the Roswell Manufacturing Company, added a brick machine shop to the mill complex on Vickery's Creek around 1853. (*Photo of the machine shop by Barney Cook*)

By 1854 Roswell Manufacturing Company was operating the largest cotton mills in north Georgia. Investors such as Henry Atwood and John Dunwody were realizing more than a ten percent annual return on their investment, according to one report.

In addition to its two cotton mills, Roswell Manufacturing Company owned the Lebanon flour mill, previously owned by part-Cherokee businessman Charles Wexford. The company employed nearly three hundred workers in various enterprises.

In 1860 the company store occupied a two-story brick and rough-hewn timber building to the east of Roswell's town square. Today this building houses an elegant restaurant called The Public House. In spite of its contemporary lighting, white linen, and potted ferns, the dining room retains the flavor of a retail establishment and the sense of once having stocked all kinds of wares on shelves that lined its rough, redbrick walls.

A guest familiar with the history of Roswell might almost expect to see Mrs. Barrington (Catherine Nephew) King, Mrs. Eliza Hand, or one of the spinners or reelers from the mill stepping up to the counter to charge a bottle of liniment or a bonnet ribbon to a company account. It seems possible a clerk might appear at any minute to mount the stairway in search of fresh tobacco for mill weaver boss Jonathan Kershaw or factory hand John R. Kendley.

While Roswell King established his mill and landowner colony, the Kendley family was busy farming in Jackson County, Georgia. John Wesley Kendley first won a land lottery in 1827, drawing a tract in what became Muscogee County, a western area of the state where Columbus, Georgia, and Phenix City, Alabama, now share suburbs. Kendley won this tract the year before Benjamin Parks's discovery spawned the gold rush in the north Georgia mountains and while the Cherokee were still determined to remain in Georgia.

In 1827 John Wesley Kendley had been married to Mary Evans for about two years and had a year-old son named William.

John Wesley and Mary Evans were devout members of the Methodist faith, which had been active in America since 1771. His name leaves little doubt that his parents also were staunch Methodists. His parents named their son after the founder of Methodism, John Wesley, who visited the eastern coast of Georgia as an Anglican missionary from 1735 to 1738.

In 1832, Kendley's luck continued in the same lottery that attracted Sweetwater Creek prospector Phillip J. Crask and the wealthy entrepreneur Roswell King. State officials drew the names of all three men from the same wheel in Milledgeville. Kendley's name matched with Lot 359 in District 13 of Section 1 (South) and also with Lot 84 in District 21 of Section 2. Unlike Crask and King, Kendley probably didn't travel all the way to Milledgeville for the actual drawing since he lived in Jackson County.

Kendley most likely waited until copies of the *Gold and Land Lottery Register* were delivered to the Jackson County Courthouse. He would have paid five dollars for his copy and had a literate friend run a finger down the pages and point out his two listings. John Kendley was not an educated man and often signed legal papers with an "X." It was an era when spelling was anything but standardized, and his name appears in various records as "Kinley," "Kenley," "Kiney," and "Kendley."

The Kendleys possibly never lived on or prospected the Muscogee County land they won in 1827. It was not a requirement to live on or cultivate land won in lotteries, and the Kendleys may have sold the eighteen-dollar grant to an agent or speculator for resale.

While Andrew Jackson and the Georgia Legislature collaborated to move the Cherokee out of Georgia, John Wesley and Mary Evans Kendley tended their farm and raised a large family to help them with chores. Daughters Elizabeth, Matilda, Catherine, and Sara Jane followed William into the family in 1828, 1831, 1833, and 1835.

The Kendleys no doubt envisioned themselves living out their years on their farm in Jackson County or on a similar farm won in a lottery. They viewed their lives as relatively uncomplicated and expected to follow God's intended pattern—they would grow old while their children, their children's spouses, and eventually their grandchildren were living and farming close by.

Sometime between 1840 and 1850, however, the lives of the Kendley family deviated from that intended pattern. They left Jackson County and moved near Roswell in Cobb County. Kendley family descendants do not know why the family made this move, but it is likely that they were simply settling the second land lot they won in 1832. By the 1840s people no longer considered Cobb County "Indian territory," and John Wesley and Mary Evans Kendley probably felt their land was safe for farming and raising their growing family.

On September 18, 1850, the census taker for Cobb County entered the Kendley family in his record. It shows John Wesley Kendley, forty-eight at the time, was still a farmer. His wife, Mary, was forty-one. William, their firstborn, was a young man working as a laborer—perhaps working at the cotton mill in Roswell. The other Kendley children—three sons and five daughters—ranged in age from twenty-two to less than a year old.

Descendants of the Kendley family have exhaustively searched Georgia historical records to piece together what happened to their great-great-grandfather, John Wesley Kendley, and his wife, Mary Evans Kendley, during the 1850s. Great-great-grandson George Howard Kendley, of Marietta, Georgia, thinks they died and were buried in an unrecorded place. "They simply disappeared from the Georgia census records between 1850 and 1860," he says, poring over genealogy-filled file folders scattered across his dining room table.

By the night in 1860 when the stars fell and Walter Stewart stood on the banks of Sweetwater Creek and spoke of the coming war, the children of John Wesley and Mary Evans Kendley in Roswell were millworkers and no longer farming. They were hourly wage earners in the factory system launched by England's Industrial Revolution the century before. We do not know exactly how or why they made this transition. But if John Wesley and Mary Evans Kendley had died, it is not difficult to imagine their daughters and sons desperately trying to earn money any way they could.

Archibald Smith moved his family to Roswell from south Georgia and established his Smith Plantation a mile north of the town square. In 1981, descendant James Skinner discovered the papers of Henry Merrell, an early assistant agent for the Roswell Manufacturing Company, in a drawer in this house. *(Sketch by Ernest DeVane used with permission of the Smith Plantation Home)*

Elizabeth, the oldest daughter, maintained the family household. At that time in 1860, she was thirty-two years old and unmarried. Living with her, perhaps in one of "The Old Bricks" apartment buildings on the flat rise above the Vickery's Creek mill gorge in Roswell, were her younger sisters Sara Jane, age twenty-five, and Mary, age seventeen, as well as her younger brothers, Thomas Hugh, age twelve, and George, age eleven. All five family members staked their future with Roswell Manufacturing Company cotton mills when the South began to rear up defiantly and prepare for war.

In the first half of the nineteenth century, children between the ages of seven and twelve made up one-third of the workforce in the United States. In some states, laws limited their workdays to ten hours, but many adults believed idleness only led to evil among children. Although Thomas Hugh and George Kendley never became as famous as Andrew Carnegie and David Livingstone, their existence was similar to these well-known men as they approached their teenage years. Industrialist and humanitarian Andrew Carnegie worked as a bobbin boy in a cotton mill in Allegheny, Pennsylvania, while missionary and explorer David Livingstone worked as a child factory hand in a Scotland cotton mill before going to Africa in 1841. Thomas Hugh and George worked in the Roswell cotton mill alongside other Roswell children such as Tuccorah (Cora), Lucenia Moore, Sarah C. James, and Savannah Reeves.

Matilda, the second-oldest Kendley daughter, married James M. Anderson in the 1850s and was raising four children. In 1860, she was listed as a factory hand at the Roswell cotton mill, although she may have left that position by the time Fort Sumter was fired upon and the Roswell Guard was formed.

Twenty-four-year-old John Robert Kendley also left the family household by 1860 and worked at the Roswell cotton mill. He married Susan Faulkner, and they had a daughter, Julia.

William, the oldest of the Kendley children, does not appear in the 1860 census for the state of Georgia. Family descendants do not know what happened to him

The Kendley brothers and sisters could not have anticipated in 1860 how much their lives would change in the following years or how far away from home some of them would be living when the Civil War finally came to an end.

CHAPTER 3

A LEGITIMATE MILITARY TARGET

Walter Stewart and A. J. White watched with growing apprehension as the superintendents at Sweetwater Creek prepared for war. As early as May 1860, William John Russell and Arnoldus Vanderhorst Brumby began to convert the civilian New Manchester mill into a military-supply format. They leased Governor Charles McDonald's interest for a period of five years, with the standard legal promise that they would return his property in as good condition as they had received it. Brumby and Russell enacted this lease agreement when many Georgians continued to believe the war would never last long enough to create rubble and refugees in their own state. These two men no doubt expected to fulfill the terms of their legal agreement as far as the condition of the property was concerned.

The names Brumby and Russell weave through Georgia history in many ways, especially in the counties where Sweetwater Creek, Roswell, and Marietta are located. As a young man, Brumby was appointed to the U.S. Military Academy at West Point, where one of his classmates was a red-haired young man from Lancaster, Ohio, named William Tecumseh Sherman. Family members and those who knew Sherman well sometimes called him "Cump."

"Cump" Sherman and Arnoldus Brumby knew each other at West Point but were not in the same class. After graduation Sherman embarked on a rather undistinguished career in the U.S. Army as an artillery lieutenant and spent a brief period on assignment near Marietta. While off duty, Sherman wandered the surrounding hills and valleys with a sketchpad, observing Indian mounds and other landmarks without suspecting how useful they would become later in his career. The twin peaks of Kennesaw Mountain stood in the background as Sherman rambled through the Marietta countryside.

Sherman resigned his first army commission in 1853 to enter the banking business in San Francisco. When the bank failed, he practiced law with two of his brothers-in-law in Leavenworth, Kansas. Shortly after, he gave that up, headed south, and became superintendent of the Louisiana State Seminary of Learning and Military Academy at Pineville. The academy later became Louisiana State University in Baton Rouge.

Athough Sherman liked the South and found Louisiana's mild, humid climate good for the asthma that plagued him, he resigned his position at the Louisiana academy in January 1861 when he was asked to sign a receipt for arms surrendered to southern rebels by the U.S. arsenal in Baton Rouge. Sherman felt unable to commit to an act he considered hostile to the Union, so he left what was quickly becoming rebel territory and traveled to St. Louis, where he managed a city streetcar company for several months before being appointed a colonel in the Thirteenth U.S. Infantry on May 14, 1861.

Sherman's West Point acquaintance Arnoldus Brumby was able to combine personal charm with executive ability and wisdom. After graduation from the military academy, he served in the U.S. Army during the Seminole War and retired from active duty to practice and teach law and civil engineering in Alabama before moving to Georgia. Like Sherman, Brumby also became the superintendent of a military academy, Georgia Military Institute, which was founded in Marietta in 1851 and modeled after West Point.

Charles J. McDonald, former governor of Georgia and principal stockholder in the New Manchester mill, was one of the stockholders in this privately chartered military institution. The faculty included Brumby's younger brother, Richard Trapier Brumby. Richard Brumby moved his family from South Carolina to Marietta, and his daughter, Rebecca Harriet, married William J. Russell, also a stockholder in the New Manchester mill.

During the thirteen years Georgia Military Institute existed in Marietta, much of the town's social life centered around the academy. On Friday evenings, cadets in dress uniform and young ladies in bobbing hoopskirts attended balls and "hops" on campus. Among those cadets were sons of some of the most prominent families in Georgia, including the son of the state's wartime governor, Joseph E. Brown. Archie Smith, son of Archibald and Anne Magill Smith of Roswell, also attended the institute.

Following afternoon drill on the parade ground in front of the white pillars of the institute's main building, Arnoldus Brumby often marched the cadets to the gardens in his private backyard at The Hedges. Admiring townspeople followed the young men in their smart, gray wool uniforms and joined them for refreshments served in the rose garden. The Hedges, a stately Greek Revival cottage, later was renamed Brumby Hall in honor of the institute's first superintendent.

Brumby remained superintendent of Georgia Military Institute until the summer of 1859, when he went to New Manchester to put the cotton mill on a military footing. Major F. W. Capers of South Carolina took over as the academy's new superintendent.

In the mid-1800s the institute stood guard on a rise outside the square in Marietta. Local residents often referred to it as "the hill." The town was formed in 1834 and began attracting tourists who, like the friends of Roswell King, traveled north every summer to escape the steamy, malaria-laden air of south Georgia. The planter families who came to Marietta for its therapeutic springs and mild climate turned the town into a thriving summer resort.

As war turned into a fact of daily life in more southern cities, the New Manchester mill on Sweetwater Creek steadily increased the amounts of yarn and osnaburg it supplied for the troops. Eventually, it became an official contractor for the Confederate government. The Confederate Congress passed exemption laws as early as 1862 to excuse superintendents and millworkers in wool- and cotton-manufacturing establishments from military service. Superintendent Josiah Welch and overseer Henry Lovern were exempt because of their positions at the New Manchester mill. Young S. H. Causey thought he would be drafted anyway because his job wasn't important enough to keep him out of the military. His older brother had already enlisted.

S. H. Causey was sixteen years old and working in the spinning room when the bosses told him and several other younger millworkers to go to Marietta so they could be mustered into Confederate military service. Causey agreed and made the trip, probably in one of the wagons loaded with goods from the mill for the Confederate Army. But he was sent back to Sweetwater Creek. The military wanted him in the spinning room at the New Manchester mill, transforming cotton fiber into yarn that could be woven into fabric for uniforms and tents.

About this time a store that sold liquor opened near New Manchester mill. Superintendent Welch went to Russell and Brumby, persuading them to buy the land so they could put the store out of business. Perhaps Welch took this action because of Cicero Tippens, a spinner at the mill who, twenty years earlier, was a factory boy under Henry Merrell in Roswell. Tippens knew the mill machinery inside and out. But Merrell learned years earlier that Tippens had a frustrating habit of drinking and neglecting business. Welch probably didn't want Tippens—or any of the other millworkers—to have easy access to alcoholic spirits.

In *Destruction of New Manchester, Georgia: The Story Behind the Ruins at Sweetwater Creek State Park,* Monroe M. King says Tippens was a good worker but liked his liquor. He appeared before the minister and the congregation of a local church several times to be saved from "Old Demon Rum." Somehow, he continued to find a source for overindulging himself even after Welch shut down the new store.

Monroe King, who lives in Douglasville, Georgia, has traced the background of Sweetwater Creek for many years. His pamphlet, on sale in the ranger's office at Sweetwater Creek State Park, paints life in the milltown as it might have been at the time of the Civil War. He describes workers gathering on Sundays for three-hour prayer meetings and sending their children to a Sunday school, which also was used to teach reading, writing, and arithmetic. King speculates that on Sunday afternoons and mill holidays, workers and their families went swimming and fishing upstream behind the dam.

Millworkers put in more than the average of 10.6 hours per day that most industry and commerce workers put in at the time of the Civil War. Sometimes, with lamps lighted, Sweetwater Creek employees put in even longer days that stretched well beyond sunset. But they also enjoyed extra days off when low water or flooding kept the waterwheel from turning. And sometimes they had impromptu holidays when the waterwheel or the dam needed repair.

By 1862 New Manchester mill had survived two fires — one caused by a match dropped into loose cotton, and the other caused by friction in the system of shafts and pulleys that powered the machinery. The loose cotton was piled in a top-floor workroom of the mill, perhaps in the picker room. Workers opened the bales, loosened the fibers, and cleaned piles of cotton, flattening them into laps of batting. Workers used two pickers and a device called a willow that was fitted with a spiked drum revolving inside a chamber, to open and clean the unprocessed cotton.

The picker room also housed the governor, which regulated the waterwheel's speed and evened out the amount of water flowing into the millrace from Sweetwater Creek. A strong surge could exert great strain on the machinery. Any time the mill was shut down because of irregular water flow, it took three days to get it operating again.

In 1862 the card room at the New Manchester mill had four sets of cards—a total of twenty-seven or twenty-eight—that workers used to straighten the tangled fibers of cotton into thin webs. They ran the laps of cotton over cylinders covered with bent-wire teeth that chewed the cotton until it was straight and smooth. Henry Lovern, the card room's overseer, supervised women who fed the webs of smooth fibers through a funnel that molded the fibers into a sliver—a long, rope-like strand about as thick as a person's finger.

The card room also housed drawing frames that drew out six slivers at a time and combined them into a single strand, or roving, also about the thickness of a human finger. A roving frame then twisted the sliver, stretching it into a thinner strand.

Workers carried the twisted cotton slivers from the card room to the spinning room on the floor below. In 1862 the spinning room contained fourteen old spinning frames and four new ones. The "mechanized" spinning process was almost one hundred years old when it was used at Sweetwater Creek. Before that, women made yarn at spinning wheels in their homes. At New Manchester, Cicero Tippens and other spinners ran machines to draw out the slivers over and over again and twist them into yarns of the sizes called for in the weaving process. As the yarns were produced, they were wound onto huge bobbins that strong young workers like S. H. Causey carried to the weave room.

The weave room had forty looms and a boiler with pipes that carried heat to the spinning room. On each loom the warp yarns— the ones given more twist during spinning so they could withstand strain—were fastened onto rollers. Some of the threads were lifted, and some were lowered so the weft threads could be driven in between by the shuttle. Over and over the shuttle drove the weft threads up between the warp threads, which then reversed their upper and lower positions before the next thrust of the shuttle. The process created fabric called gray goods that were bleached and dyed as ordered.

A. J. White worked in one of these rooms at the mill until he enlisted in a Confederate unit called the Banks Partisan Rangers and went to fight the Yankees. In June 1862 he had just completed a journey from Atlanta through Macon and was stationed in a military camp on the banks of the Vernon River, fourteen miles southwest of Savannah. Seated under an oak tree outside his tent door, he wrote to his wife, Margaret, who was still living in New Manchester with their two small children.

"Margaret, I would give all I possess if I could be back with you and the children and could stay with you," he wrote. "I know that I can never want to see you and them any worse than I do now." A. J. White went on to describe his view of the "broad Atlantick Ocean" and promised he would "telgraph" if he got sick.

We do not know if Margaret White was working in the mill in 1862 when she received this letter. Folded carefully, it was post-marked "Savannah Ga." over a Jefferson Davis stamp. Most likely she was not working then, but became a millworker sometime during the next two years as more men left Sweetwater Creek to defend the South.

The summer of 1863 took Walter Washington Stewart and the Campbell Salt Springs Guards west to Vicksburg to help defend the South's last best stronghold against Union control of the Mississippi River. Situated on a steep bluff overlooking the rolling waters, Vicksburg was expected to defy any possible attack. With the aid of units such as the Campbell Salt Springs Guards, the city stubbornly endured a stranglehold siege of more than six weeks before Confederate commanders surrendered their forces to Ulysses S. Grant.

Arnoldus Brumby's old West Point friend, William T. Sherman, also was in Vicksburg. He had been promoted to Major General of Volunteers after his successful leadership in the Battle of Shiloh in April 1862. He was serving under Grant when Vicksburg drew a last exhausted breath and surrendered on July 4, 1863.

Union forces won the siege at Vicksburg logistically, but lost more than ten thousand men to the Confederacy's nine thousand. Many in the South viewed this defeat as a tragedy that would prolong the war, which they earlier had hoped would come to a swift, victorious conclusion.

Among thirty-one thousand Confederate soldiers captured during the final operations at Vicksburg were at least thirty-five

A. J. White, who served with the Banks Partisan Rangers, wrote this letter to his wife, Margaret, from Savannah on June 13, 1862. Margaret was sent north with her children by Union troops in July 1864. Although she returned to the Sweetwater Creek area following the war, her husband died near Chattanooga, Tennessee, before he could return. *(Letter from the Andrew J. White Papers used with permission of the Rare Book, Manuscript, and Special Collections Library at Duke University)*

members of the Campbell Salt Springs Guards, including Walter Stewart. Like many prisoners captured before 1864, Stewart was paroled just two days after his capture when he agreed to sign a statement saying he would not fight again. Once he signed the statement and obtained his parole, however, he returned to his unit and continued to fight.

Sometime after his parole, Walter Stewart returned to New Manchester on furlough to visit his wife, Lizzie, and children. When he arrived Stewart discovered that Lizzie was not working inside the cotton mill as he had thought she would. Her widowed mother, Elizabeth Webb Russell, came to live with Lizzie and the children along with their Uncle James who had rheumatism and could not fight. Mrs. Russell would not hear of her daughter working in the mill. Instead, she persuaded Lizzie to set up a loom in the house at the farm and take in piecework to make ends meet.

Lizzie and the children were overjoyed at Walter's visit. Seeing him still able-bodied was a comfort when so many of the mill men were limping home or sending weak messages from field hospitals. They listened with sad hearts when he told them about the terrible sacrifices of Vicksburg women and children.

Walter was unable to stay, and Synthia Catherine wished she could go with him when he returned to his unit. When he marched off this second time, the family was growing older. Sarah was eleven and Synthia Catherine nine. Jim was six, Linnie Isabella four, and Jeff Davis, two.

Before kissing Lizzie and the children goodbye, Walter told them, "If the Yankees ever get to Atlanta, I'm coming home. I've been in this war long enough now. Don't you worry. I'll come home and protect you unless they kill me or take me prisoner again." As her father left to return to his unit, Synthia Catherine tucked his promise away in her mind, hoping the Yankees would never reach Atlanta.

Each year of the war—as with all long wars—daily life became increasingly more difficult for civilians and soldiers. Increasing prices for food and clothing, along with the scarcity of some items, began to plague Georgia by 1863. That spring, New Manchester experienced a "woman seizure" when a group of women stopped a wagon driven from the Sweetwater Creek mill to a storage facility in Marietta. The women overpowered the driver and seized several bales of cotton yarn, probably so they could clothe their families.

Many of the male employees of the New Manchester cotton mill were still exempt from military service in the fall of 1863, but formed their own cavalry unit—Company D, Second Regiment—of the State Troops so they would be prepared if war or other troubles came to their doorstep. They nicknamed their unit the Rebel Rangers and held drills even though they were not issued arms or ammunition.

Georgia's wartime governor, Joseph E. Brown, could sense Union troops gathering on the Tennessee horizon in late 1863 as well as anyone else could. Reluctantly, he considered the possibility that troops would invade Georgia and so ordered a census of all able-bodied men not serving in the Confederate Army. Men such as John Akin and John Alexander, George Denney and Cicero Tippens appear on this census list for the Sweetwater Creek area. They became prime candidates for conscription in spite of their positions at the mill.

Arnoldus Brumby had been the largest stockholder of New Manchester Manufacturing Company since Charles McDonald's death in 1860. The McDonald family holdings were diluted because Charles McDonald's will directed that his stock be divided among his heirs. Brumby now became president of the company too.

Brumby, an experienced instructor from Georgia Military Institute, found it challenging to run a cotton mill during the Civil War. Early in 1864 the Confederate Congress repealed exemption laws for textile millworkers and superintendents, but those drafted still could be detailed to work in the mills if the military was convinced the need was great enough. For the first part of the year, New Manchester Manufacturing Company on Sweetwater Creek remained Campbell County's largest employer and posted its largest payroll.

In January 1864, Arnoldus Brumby wrote to Governor Brown, complaining that armed mobs were robbing the mill wagons full of cotton fabric and yarn on their way to storage locations in Marietta and Atlanta. "I enclose an affidavit from our Superintendent, Mr. J. Welch, in regard to armed mobs which have robbed us of our property and are now assembling in such force as to make it impossible to carry on our work with any security even of life unless the State can in some way protect us," Brumby wrote. "We have sued in damages & have prosecuted all the parties we could find who robbed our wagons some time back, but this seems to have no good effect."

Brumby told the governor that the cavalry company formed by the millworkers had arms and ammunition to protect the mill against mobs, but the governor would have to decide how to protect the wagons. The mill could not function if it had to send out its few remaining men to guard the wagons.

There is no record of Brown's reply to Brumby's letter. By 1864, Georgians were swamping Brown with requests for protection and for relief from impossibly difficult circumstances. People wrote to him as they would to an older relative, telling him about their sufferings and begging for his help. The governor received more requests than he could meet.

In February 1864, New Manchester mill supervisor William John Russell concluded that joining the militia was the best way to defend Georgia. He enlisted as a private on February 26 and sent Rebecca and the rest of his family away from the Atlanta area. More than sixty years later, their grandson was elected governor of Georgia.

As 1864 trudged on, the number of male workers dwindled steadily in Georgia textile mills. In many places, including New Manchester and Roswell, the labor force became a random mix of men who could not fight or were still exempt, as well as women, children, and occasionally slaves. Confederate quartermaster officers proposed that prisoners of war work in the mills to keep cloth and rope production up. This suggestion, however, met raised eyebrows and outright rejection. Some superintendents were afraid Yankee prisoners would sabotage production. Others were convinced female workers would rebel if even one Yankee soldier came to work in a Georgia textile plant.

Synthia Catherine Stewart's daughter, Pearl Boyd Bruce, recalled that Lizzie walked to the New Manchester mill during the last hour or so of production each workday afternoon in 1864. Because Lizzie had some education with numbers, she could add and make a daily record of the work done in the mill. Each evening Lizzie counted the work and prepared a report for the Confederate government.

It was oppressively hot that summer, and perhaps Lizzie took along Sarah and Synthia Catherine on her afternoon walks down to the mill. Together they could enjoy the cooler shade as they descended toward the noisy, spraying waters of Factory Shoals on Sweetwater Creek. And they could hear the towhees screaming overhead, "Drink your teeeee! Drink your teeee!" and see the red-tailed hawks catching the thermals in the clear blue skies above the waters.

The mill they walked to each afternoon had become a legitimate military target. New Manchester Manufacturing Company became a contractor for the Confederacy as early as 1861, and the strategists who gathered information for advancing Union troops were well aware of its existence. Further jeopardizing people in New Manchester was the strategically located bridge at Ferguson's Crossing, near the mill. It was the last bridge across Sweetwater Creek before it emptied into the Chattahoochee River just a mile or two downstream.

When Abraham Lincoln promoted Ulysses S. Grant to chief commander of the armies of the United States, William Tecumseh Sherman assumed command of all troops in the western theater. Sherman's first significant orders were to move against Atlanta, and he began this relentless push from Chattanooga, Tennessee, in May 1864.

For five months General Joseph Johnston's army was posted about thirty miles southeast of Chattanooga. Sherman planned to follow Grant's orders—attack Johnston's forces, break them apart, and charge as far as possible into Confederate territory, doing as much damage as possible to enemy resources along the way.

Sherman did not organize a timetable for this campaign, but developed his philosophy of "total war" as he prepared to invade Georgia. To him, "total war" meant making life as miserable for civilians as for the military and keeping the countryside and the people from providing any support for the Confederate military forces. The rumor mill in some parts of the state put out the word that Sherman was determined to sit down to dinner and celebrate Independence Day, 1864, in a conquered Atlanta.

Joe Johnston put up a good fight. He even defeated Sherman and his troops during a rainy two-week siege at Kennesaw Mountain before the Union general ever ate a bite in Atlanta, but the Confederate forces were never able to hold Sherman off long enough to gather strength. Atlanta held out until the end of August, but from May forward it was clear that Union troops would push relentlessly to cross the Chattahoochee River. They were slowed somewhat by the spring rains that had swollen the river well beyond its normal shallow depths, but soon summer weather would bring the river back down to fordable proportions.

Accounts printed in northern newspapers, telegraphed by correspondents in the field, show that Union soldiers came to view the Chattahoochee as the last great obstacle in their path to the defiant southern city of Atlanta.

When Sherman sat down to write the comprehensive report about his campaign against Atlanta, he remembered himself as particularly sensitive to the cruelty of the destruction he was about to cause. Perhaps he felt that way because of his service in the area twenty years earlier, when he had carried his sketchpad and wandered the countryside near Marietta. Or perhaps he felt that way because of his classmate Arnoldus Brumby, who shared some of the same experiences as a young man.

"The scene was enchanting," Sherman wrote of the Kennesaw Mountain and Marietta area in an official report dated September 15, 1864. "Too beautiful to be disturbed by the harsh clamor of war; but the Chattahoochee lay beyond, and I had to reach it."

On the last day of June, in a decidedly desolate mood, Sherman wrote to his wife, Ellen, to tell her of his plans for Atlanta and his feelings about them. "I begin to regard the death and mangling of a couple thousand men as a small affair, a kind of morning dash— and it may be well that we become so hardened."

For Sherman the harsh clamor of war was about to focus, at least briefly, on civilian women and children. What did Ellen Sherman think about her husband's attitude toward southern civilians? Would she have approved of his determination to turn thousands of them into refugees in his efforts to devastate his enemy? Would she have understood if she had learned that he would soon order the deportation of hundreds of women and children for simply doing their jobs?

At the end of June, Johnston withdrew his troops from his fortified line at Kennesaw Mountain in spite of his victory there, and retreated south through Marietta. Johnston's purpose in shifting his forces, as Sherman correctly supposed, was to defend the Confederate railroad crossings and the Chattahoochee River. But his actions also left New Manchester, Roswell, and many other towns west of Atlanta, wide open to attack.

Johnston pessimistically believed there was little he could do to stop Sherman. He overestimated the size of the Union forces. Still, he told Governor Brown that he could keep the enemy north of the Chattahoochee for a long time—perhaps even a month or more.

As soon as Johnston withdrew from Kennesaw and began his retreat south, Josiah Welch, who was left in charge of the mill on Sweetwater Creek, concluded he and his workers would soon find themselves in the path of Sherman's forces. Charles McDonald was dead by this time. William John Russell was a private in the militia, and Arnoldus Brumby had left to serve as colonel of the Fourteenth Georgia Regiment.

On June 28 Welch decided it was time to safeguard the assets of the mill from Union troops. He cleaned out the company safe, which is said to have contained Confederate currency and certificates valued between ninety and a hundred thousand dollars, and prepared to leave New Manchester. He left Henry Lovern, age twenty-seven, who was overseer of the card room, and head spinner Cicero Tippens, age thirty-three, in charge of the mill; he told them to keep it running and churning out military supplies as long as possible. Then, like many other Atlanta-area property owners and managers, Welch fled.

CHAPTER 4

EDGINESS IN ROSWELL

The war first delivered personal fear to Roswell civilians one night in early September 1863, when Union and Confederate troops fought on Georgia soil, struggling for control of Chattanooga, Tennessee. Young Katana King wrote to her cousins and friends down near the sea island plantations that everyone she knew in Roswell had packed up what they could during the night, afraid they might have to flee for their lives. But scouts reported that the enemy was driven off in a different direction, and everyone relaxed a little—at least for the time being.

Residents of Roswell were edgy after the Union attack on Charleston in July. By August there was talk of putting up fortifications around the town and barricading the street near Great Oaks, Dr. Pratt's home. The residents had at least two cannons and numerous small arms on hand.

Roswell was not untouched by the war. Like Sweetwater Creek, the town sent many of its own—both landowners and millworkers— to do battle as members of Confederate regiments. Matilda Kendley Anderson, the second-oldest Kendley daughter, lost her husband James in 1861. He was wounded in battle, captured, and died of his wounds in a Union prison camp. Matilda started working in the cotton mill to support their four children.

Matilda's brother, John Robert, joined the Roswell Guard as a corporal when the unit was formed in early 1861. He was promoted to sergeant before he, too, was wounded and captured. The Roswell Guard fought under Captain Thomas E. King at First Manassas in Virginia, where King was wounded. Hugh Proudfoot, the Roswell Manufacturing Company bookkeeper, also served in the guard unit.

When John Robert Kendley was captured, he did what Walter Stewart had done in Vicksburg: He took the oath not to fight against the Union and was released. Instead of immediately rejoining the Confederate troops, Kendley returned to Roswell and worked in the cotton mill with his sisters and brothers. In June 1863, millworkers ages sixteen to sixty formed the Roswell Battalion to defend their town. John Robert, as Walter Stewart had done earlier, ignored his Union oath and joined the battalion. He entered as third lieutenant, probably because he was one of the few millworkers with prior military experience. Most of the unit's members were "detailed men" from the mills who were exempted from regular Confederate service.

Six of Barrington King's eight sons served in the Confederate military. Five of them served with the Roswell Guard, the Roswell Battalion, or the Roswell Troopers, organized by Barrington King Jr. in March 1862. Sons of other prominent Roswell families also served the Confederacy, including James Dunwody Bulloch, a naval agent in England who supervised building the raider ship *Alabama*.

Only one week after the nighttime scare that woke Roswell residents, the King family suffered its first casualty of the war. Captain Thomas E. King was wounded and died at Chickamauga while riding as volunteer aide to Brigadier General Preston Smith during his first night on the battlefield.

"But oh! How glorious to die for one's Country," wrote Josephine Clay Habersham in her diary when news reached Savannah that her brother-in-law, Thomas King, had been killed. "I can imagine no higher destiny for a noble-minded man."

At that time the oldest son, Charles Barrington King, was serving as minister of the White Bluff Presbyterian Church near Savannah. As a boy, Charles worked for Henry Merrell in the cotton mills after school and later studied at Princeton Theological Seminary. Josephine wrote in her diary that Charles was overcome with grief at the news of his brother Thomas's death. He left White Bluff and traveled first to the battlefield, twelve miles south of Chattanooga, to learn more about what had happened to his brother and then to Roswell to comfort his grieving parents and his widowed sister-in-law, Mary Read Clemens King, and her three children. Josephine noted that Charles didn't preach that Sunday or the next and that he looked terrible when he finally returned to the pulpit later in October.

Barrington King sent a family slave to the battlefield to bring home his son's body. The slave made a stretcher from the side of a wagon to carry the body back to Roswell.

Captain James Roswell King assumed command of Thomas's Roswell Battalion. When time permitted he drilled his men and directed them to erect fortifications on the main road from Roswell to Marietta.

During the fall of 1863 many of the landowner women of Roswell busied themselves preparing lint bandages and other medical supplies for the hundreds of wounded Confederate soldiers in Marietta and Atlanta. James L. and Arthur Skinner, who have collected and edited letters written by members of the Archibald Smith family, state that the Smiths seriously considered evacuating their Roswell farm property and heading south to "safer" areas of Georgia as early as September 1863.

The Skinners also tell us in their book, *The Death of a Confederate*, that Barrington King was determined to stage a standoff against Union intruders. Mrs. Archibald Smith wrote in September that "Mr. King says he does not intend to move until the Yankees actually set fire to his house, but when that comes he may not find it an easy matter to get away, tho' he has plenty of carriages & horses & plenty of money to replace their comforts even if every thing in his house is destroyed."

During the years of the Civil War, news spread primarily through letters circulated among family members. Without radio or television and with more and more daily newspapers suspending operation as the war began its rampage through Georgia, letters often provided the best means of communicating what was happening on a day-to-day basis. We know a fair amount about the tragedies and heartbreaks of the prominent citizens of Roswell because they had the time and the education to correspond with each other. On the other hand we know very little about tragedies such as the death of Matilda Kendley Anderson's husband, primarily because most of the town's millworkers lacked the ability to read or write, and those who were literate had little time for composing letters.

In November 1863 Roswell residents received ominous news of Union victories at Lookout Mountain and Missionary Ridge. The Confederates lost the battle for Chattanooga, and all of Georgia shuddered as the Confederate Army evacuated Tennessee and retreated southward. Even so, the residents of Roswell and Sweetwater Creek did not feel a pervading sense of defeat. Their mills were still producing record amounts of textile supplies and at the time may even have been expanding operations.

On December 28, 1863, Barrington King Jr. requested a thirty-day leave of absence from his military assignment in Virginia to return to Roswell. He stated that he ordered machinery imported from England to update his cotton and woolen mills and he wanted to go home long enough to oversee its installation.

"The machines are not in operation, my *personal attention* being necessary to put them in full & successful operation, thereby advancing the interest of our *whole* country, as well as *personal*," King wrote in his application for leave. He reminded his superior officers that "By the Act of Congress [of the Confederacy]" he could have been exempted completely from military service and stayed at home to supervise his machinery. "But my *first* & *greatest* duty is for my country, and all I ask, is to [be] allowed the above time *now* that I may be able to serve my *own* interest as well as my *country's*."

The back of King's application for leave, preserved in the archives of the Atlanta History Center, indicates that his request was approved on December 29. He had not been home to Roswell for an entire year.

Researcher James Skinner suggests it would have been extremely difficult for new machinery to have reached Roswell in 1863 because of the Union blockades of all southern ports. Either the machinery had been shipped before the war and just never installed, or Barrington King was simply looking for a reasonable excuse to request leave and visit home.

The early months of 1864 were unusually cold and wet in Roswell. Heavy sleet and snow fell as late as the last week of March, and the azaleas were not in full bloom until the middle of May. The choices of foods kept shrinking as the months went by, and some accounts refer to people eating little else but bacon with rice or corn.

During May 1864 rumors and news of Sherman's victories within Georgia began to reach Roswell almost daily. Sherman had troops in Dalton on May 14, in Resaca on May 15, and Adairsville on May 17.

On May 19 Captain James Roswell King received a warning from Confederate Adjutant A. W. Harris that Roswell might be the focus of a Union cavalry raiding party. The Adjutant was not concerned about an all-out attack, but he was worried that raiders might seize artillery and ammunition stockpiled at Roswell. "They would not, likely, bring artillery with them, and should they get possession of yours, it would enable them greatly to damage us here," Harris wrote to James King from Atlanta.

Harris also passed along a directive from a Colonel Wright. "If a Union cavalry raid should be too large to resist, the Confederate soldiers stationed at Roswell should fall back to the Atlanta side of the Chattahoochee and burn the bridge across the river."

James King not only delivered this message to the military personnel stationed at Roswell, but he also began to make preparations for how the Ivy Woolen Mill should be managed if the Yankees came to town. "I left the mill in charge of my head man & told them [& the Hands] to remain at their post or in their houses until driven out & to protect the property if they could."

The "head man" James King referred to was probably either Olney Eldridge or Samuel Bonfoy—both men were superintendents of the mill at that time. The "hands" were the men, women, and children who worked as carders, weavers, reelers, and spinners in the workrooms on the various floors of the woolen mill.

Barrington King made similar preparations at Roswell Manufacturing Company's two cotton mills. In spite of his earlier determination to stand his ground, by late May Barrington King thought better of his situation and fled Roswell for Atlanta with members of his family and household servants. He took with him books and papers pertaining to the mills but decided against trying to remove any machinery. "I concluded to keep the factory in motion to the last hour," he wrote to a friend on May 30. "Mr. Eldridge will remain there [in Roswell], Mr. Camp & Ralph as long as practicable—the hands all at work."

The "Mr. Eldridge" Barrington King referred to in this letter was Olney Eldridge, superintendent of the Roswell Cotton Mills in 1864. "Mr. Camp" was certainly George Hull Camp who was chief agent of Roswell Manufacturing Company in 1864. Camp had been an assistant to Barrington King since 1849.

The workers in all three mills must have been terribly frightened to hear the rumors and watch the wagons—and every other possible means of carrying possessions—load up and pull away as member after member of the original Roswell planter families abandoned the town. The planter families fled first to Atlanta and then to whatever accommodations they could arrange in other parts of the state. The mill families had virtually no assets and certainly no means of moving out of the way of Sherman's forces.

Before he left town Barrington King decided the well-stocked supplies at the Roswell Manufacturing Company store on Atlanta Street would be safer in the hands of the factory supervisors and the employees themselves if there should actually be a raid. He directed that the two months' worth of provisions on hand be distributed to the mill families. This and other actions by the planter families must have made it clearer and clearer to Sara Jane and Mary Kendley, their two young brothers, and the other millworkers that they would have to fend for themselves if the dreaded Yankees marched into Roswell.

The Skinners' book, *The Death of a Confederate,* quotes a letter from Barrington King written from Atlanta to Archibald Smith on June 4, 1864. King wrote of "all moving on as usual at our mills yesterday, our teams hauling off the usual production from day to day." He told Smith that he sent a bale of Yarn 50 belonging to Smith to a factor in Savannah who needed directions about what to do with it.

As Sherman carried out Grant's orders to plunge deep into Confederate territory, he became concerned about preserving the supply lines to his troops that stretched by railroad from Louisville down through Nashville and then over to Chattanooga. During June

In the 1860s, the Roswell Manufacturing Company store occupied this two-story brick and rough-hewn timber building on the east side of the town square. Late in May 1864, Barrington King feared a Yankee invasion and ordered the well-stocked store closed. Provisions on hand were distributed to mill supervisors and employees. *(Photo by Barney Cook of the Public House Restaurant that now occupies this building)*

1864 he wrote U.S. Secretary of War Edwin M. Stanton and made a particularly bizarre suggestion for how to protect this supply line as he extended it even farther south.

Sherman asked Stanton for permission to send "all males and females who have encouraged or harbored guerrillas" out of the country—perhaps to places like Honduras, British or French Guiana, San Domingo, or even Lower California. "Our armies traverse the land, and waves of disaffection, sedition, and crime close in behind and our track disappears," wrote Sherman. "But one thing is certain, there is a class of people, men, women, and children, who must be killed or banished before we can hope for peace and order even as far south as Tennessee."

The Lincoln Administration in Washington denied Sherman's plan to turn "secesh sympathizers" into foreign exiles, but Lincoln did place the State of Kentucky under martial law in early July. Although Sherman's request was denied, speculation has persisted ever since he wrote that letter that he might have carried out at least part of his intentions on his own. Some have tried to link Sherman's request to colonies of southerners who settled in Brazil and other countries, but these appear to be people who chose to leave the South on their own and could afford to do so.

Kenner Dudley Garrard was thirty-seven years old when he arrived in Roswell, Georgia, in early July 1864. He studied at Harvard but left during his second year to attend West Point. He graduated eighth in the Class of 1851 at the military academy, eleven years after "Cump" Sherman.

At the time Fort Sumter was fired upon, Garrard was serving as a lieutenant of U.S. cavalry in the Southwest. Rebel Texans who were not yet officially affiliated with the Confederacy captured Garrard at San Antonio. He was paroled, exchanged in August 1862, and appointed colonel of the 146th New York. Newspaper accounts paint Garrard as a hero in the battles of Fredericksburg (December 1862), Chancellorsville (May 1863), and Gettysburg (July 1983).

In February 1864 he assumed command of the Second Cavalry Division of the Army of the Cumberland. This brought him in contact with Sherman, under whom he participated in the steady progression toward the rebel city of Atlanta.

Many descriptions of the military operations in northern Georgia in May and June 1864 suggest that Garrard thought he was not in Sherman's good graces because he had been overly cautious in carrying out a number of Sherman's orders. These descriptions suggest that Garrard was particularly determined to redeem himself by doing an outstanding job when Sherman ordered him to "draw out at once and go to Roswell" on July 4, 1864.

Sherman's main concern was that Garrard's forces should stop all Confederate attempts to sabotage the Union troops' communications. "You now understand the geography so well that I have no doubt you can prevent [General Joseph] Wheeler from doing much damage between Marietta and Allatoona," Sherman wrote in his orders to Garrard. His final direction to Garrard was to "arrest every citizen in the country whom you find likely to prove a spy, and keep moving so that your force cannot be computed."

PART II
THE CONCOMITANT
EVILS OF WAR

CHAPTER 5

EVERYONE UNDER ARREST

The unusually cool spring of 1864 gave way to sweltering temperatures by late June and early July in Georgia. The heat was so oppressive that virtually every soldier and every civilian, Confederate or Union, who recorded events during those summer months mentioned the hot weather. A late-afternoon shower on June 30 cooled the air somewhat and temporarily washed away the steamy haze hanging over Sweetwater Creek and at Vickery's Creek in Roswell, just a few miles to the northeast. By the next afternoon, though, the air was again almost too thick to breathe.

At the end of June, Sherman's branches of the Union Army were smarting a little from their losses at Kennesaw Mountain and turned their focus toward Atlanta with renewed determination. General George Stoneman, age forty-two, was directing the Cavalry Corps of the Army of the Ohio. Stoneman, a veteran of General George B. McClellan's staff in West Virginia, fought in the Peninsular campaign of 1862 and the battle of Fredericksburg. On the morning of July 2, Stoneman directed his cavalry to the west bank of Sweetwater Creek.

The primary accomplishment of Stoneman's ride downriver was that it diverted the Confederates' attention away from the major crossing attempts planned for Union troops farther north at shallow fords and bridges in places like Roswell. Few Civil War history books give more than a cursory mention of the Union encounter at Sweetwater Creek. Most do not mention it at all. This action was not, in the general scope of things, a major focus of battle or a significant scene of death.

Yet for each of the two hundred people who lived and worked in New Manchester, the arrival of the northern soldiers was a major event. They dreaded and anticipated it for months, wondering which terrible rumors about Yankees were true. They had watched mill superintendent Josiah Welch pack up and leave, and now they saw Confederate troops burn bridges and set up perfunctory defenses along the creek.

It was close to ten o'clock that Saturday morning when Union troops came within sight of the mill at Factory Shoals. The town was then officially called New Manchester, but scant Union records of this encounter consistently call it Sweetwater Creek or Factory Shoals.

The sun was heading upward, and work was proceeding at the mill as it always did on Saturdays. Young S. H. Causey was probably in the spinning room waiting for filled bobbins to carry down to the weave room. Members of the Humphries family and the Tutchstone family were probably already hard at work when someone up in the picker room first caught a glimpse of the file of men stepping toward the mill. They wore blue wool uniforms in spite of the heat. Word spread quickly from workroom to workroom and floor to floor as Stoneman's men marched closer.

To everyone's relief, no shots were fired. Major Thompkins and Colonel Adams strode into the mill office and demanded to know who was in charge. Within minutes they arrested overseers Henry Lovern and Cicero Tippens.

The order went out to round up the residents of New Manchester and bring them to the factory. "You are all under arrest," the people were told, but no one was sure exactly what that meant.

As Union soldiers approached the Causey house, S. H. Causey's mother began to panic. Her older son was home on sick leave from his Confederate unit. If the Yankees caught him, they would surely shoot him on the spot or send him to a Federal prison, and she had heard how terrible those prisons could be. "Quick!" she told her son as she sent him off into the woods so he would not be captured.

Then she and the younger children hurried to the pathway outside the mill and stood with S. H.

"Shut this mill down immediately," Colonel Adams growled at Henry Lovern. "Gather up all the bales of finished cloth and give them out to the workers. If you don't try anything foolish, nobody will get hurt." The workers, having lived with shortages for months on end, were glad for the cloth as a gesture of goodwill.

The great, groaning machines inside the mill ground to a halt as Henry Lovern carried out the colonel's order. The shafts, gears, and leather belts stopped humming. Everyone expected the soldiers to burn the mill, but that did not happen—at least not that day.

At two o'clock that afternoon Stoneman sent a dispatch declaring that he had taken a position his troops could hold against the whole rebel army if necessary, but he made no mention of plans to burn the mill on Sweetwater Creek. Major General J. M. Schofield also sent a dispatch that day stating that Stoneman took possession of the bridge (which he was repairing) at Sweetwater Town, as well as the west bank of the creek as far down as the factory.

Nine-year-old Synthia Catherine Stewart stood in the pathway outside the mill with the other residents of New Manchester. It was slightly cooler there beside the creek in the shade of the giant beech trees. Synthia Catherine saw the mountain laurel shrubs with their fading pink blooms and the lacy light-green ferns that nestled beneath them on the sloping hillside opposite the mill. A dry leaf picked that moment to break loose from a twig above her head. The air was so quiet she heard it rustle down through the tree branches and watched it flutter to the ground at her feet.

Her mother and grandmother, her Uncle James, and her sisters and brother stood with her. Sarah was twelve, Jim seven, and Linnie Isabella five. Synthia Catherine's mother, Lizzie, held the family's share of the cloth from the mill. Synthia missed poor little Jeff. It was just six weeks on this exact day since her smallest brother, the one named for the leader of the Confederacy, had died. If Jeff had lived until the weather turned this warm . . . it was still icy cold in April when he was sick. He was so small, and it was so hard to bury him.

"As soon as transportation is available you people will be moved west," the Yankee officers announced. "You will be transported out of the paths of the armies and safe from harm."

That sounded fair enough to the workers. And if the mill was not going to be burned, then perhaps they could all return and continue their lives in a few weeks.

Since the Union Army wagons would not arrive for at least two days, the officers allowed the residents to walk back to their homes under guard. The Yankee soldiers took the opportunity to search every nook and cranny of the mill and the town. They broke open the company safe but found nothing—mill superintendent Welch saw to that before he fled town. One detail of Yankees reportedly charged into the mill, tore the partially woven cloth from the looms and the threads from the spinning frames, and removed the leather belting that drove the machines. The soldiers also walked the dusty roads of town, but they did not find S. H. Causey's older brother.

Synthia Catherine walked with her family back to their farm without any inkling of what would happen next. She tried to figure out how best to cope with the family's new set of circumstances. "Will Papa come home for us now?" she wondered, remembering her father's promise.

That afternoon, as the Yankees roamed freely around town, one soldier burst into the Stewart home and helped himself to a pocketful of eggs. He didn't harm anything or anyone—he just took the eggs and left.

Although the Stewarts had little variety in their diet at this point in the Civil War, they still had a number of chickens around their farmhouse. The children's grandmother, Elizabeth Webb

Russell, decided to cook up the remaining chickens and fix one last good meal for the family before they climbed into the wooden army wagons to be carried away from home for an unknown period of time.

While their grandmother prepared the meal, the four Stewart children were out in the yard, perhaps watching warily as the Yankee soldiers cavorted up and down the road. "We had a window on each side of the fireplace," Synthia Catherine told her grandson when she recorded her memories on the phonograph record in 1947. "Grandma came to the window and told us to get ready for dinner."

Synthia Catherine and the other children scurried around the corner of the house to the shelf with the bucket and bowl of water for washing. Suddenly, no doubt in response to the hearty smell of roast chicken, the yard filled with blue-coated Yankees. "Well, lookee here, we're just in time," said one of them.

"They didn't ask if they could or not," Synthia Catherine told her grandson. "They just walked right in and sat down at Mama's table and ate up all that dinner Grandma had cooked, and we didn't have a thing left to cook another day."

After that experience, Lizzie Stewart apparently decided it was time to protect as much as she could from the Yankee intruders. As her daughter Synthia Catherine remembered it, "We took my father's clothes and packed a suit of them up a hollow tree so it wouldn't rain on them or anything. And then we took a big old water pitcher and filled it full of our silverware and set it down in a hollow stump. We couldn't put any dishes in the pitcher, so we just packed them in around the edges of the pitcher and covered them up with trash and one thing and another. And then we just went off and left them."

While the residents of New Manchester waited nervously for the appearance of Union Army wagons, General Garrard's forces invaded Roswell just a few miles to the north. On Friday, July 8, Major Thompkins told Henry Lovern that the Roswell factory mills had been burned and that he had orders from Sherman to burn the

Sweetwater Creek mill too. Thompkins ordered the millworkers to get ready immediately to travel west, where they could find provisions because they soon would not be able to find anything of value around New Manchester. "General Sherman intends to destroy everything in this part of the country," Thompkins explained to Lovern.

The eight Union soldiers assigned to burn the mill lugged huge cans of kerosene to each story. They splashed and sprinkled the flammable liquid until the mill was saturated from top to bottom, but they "considerately" doused all of the nearby dwellings with water so they would not catch fire as the mill burned. Finally they applied the match to the mill, and the wooden framework and floors inside the mill began to crackle and spit.

Then a Union officer announced, "We're also burning this store. But first you workers just go on in there and help yourselves to anything you can carry with you when you leave." Within minutes the store was virtually empty, and within an hour it burned as brightly as the mill across the road.

The pamphlet that Monroe King wrote, *Destruction of New Manchester Georgia: The Story Behind the Ruins at Sweetwater Creek Park,* suggests additional destruction occurred when Federal soldiers turned their twelve-pound guns on the wooden dam spanning the creek above the mill. Each shot, writes King, ripped great holes in the dam and sent massive timbers sailing into the air.

Based on his own research, however, Michael Hitt disagrees with Monroe King on this point. His documentation suggests that Federal officers in the area did not have large artillery with them.

In addition to burning the mill and company store on July 8, the Federal forces once again rounded up residents of New Manchester. S. H. Causey heard the officers tell the people they would not just be making a short journey into western Georgia for their safety as they were originally told. Instead, they would have two choices. Their first choice was to sign an agreement promising they would not again engage in making cloth for the Confederacy; if they signed the agreement, they could be paroled. Their second choice was to be shipped north across the Ohio River and behind Federal lines, where soldiers would set them free and allow them to work in Union mills.

Most of the families, including the Stewarts and the Causeys, decided to be shipped north. In 1932, S. H. Causey remembered it happening this way, "When my mother, who was a widow with several small children, was told that she must either sign a certificate stating that she would not help the Confederates by returning to work, or go north to find employment for herself and her children, she decided upon the latter course. There really wasn't much choice in the matter, and she reasoned that as long as we were to be allowed to earn a livelihood, we would not starve. Nearly all our neighbors were women with large families of small children dependent upon them for support, and most of them felt the same way that we did."

The millworkers at Sweetwater Creek originally may have been given a choice that included staying in Georgia if they signed an agreement not to work, but it is doubtful that option remained available on July 8. In the summer of 1864, Sherman was determined to remove any skilled laborers he could find from Georgia and other southern states until the Confederacy was defeated.

Synthia Catherine Stewart listened as a Yankee officer barked out orders. "You women get on home now and get some clothes for your children and a suit for yourselves. Don't get any more than you can carry in your arms. Don't take anything else out of your houses, only what you can carry. And then you get out of your houses and be back here by six o'clock this evening."

The officer warned residents that soldiers would burn their houses if they didn't get out by the specified time. He also told them they would have to spend the night at the meeting place if the army wagons did not arrive until the next morning. The people were to meet at six o'clock that evening by the river bridge that had been burned. The Yankees were busily repairing.

Mrs. Causey listened and worried. If the whole area was devastated, how would her other son survive, alone and sick, hiding in the woods? He would not be able to eat, and it might be weeks or months before he could find any soldiers in the area who were not Yankees. All the Confederates were retreating south and probably had already crossed the Chattahoochee River.

Mrs. Causey stepped forward. "Officer," she called out. "There is something I must tell you." She knew she might be sealing her son's death warrant, but she decided to take the chance and was rewarded for taking the risk. The officer listened quietly and told her to bring her son forward. He would have the same choice as the millworkers and would be allowed to go with his family.

Lizzie Stewart had no idea that her husband, Walter, was not far away during the week she and other New Manchester residents waited for the Union Army wagons to arrive. By that point in the war, communications between the military and civilians in the South were scanty at best, and units like the Campbell Salt Springs Guards often received orders to move without well-organized strategy.

Confederate service records of the Campbell Salt Springs Guards suggest that Stewart almost made it back to Sweetwater Creek in time to see his family before they went north. But it is unknown whether he knew what was happening to them or whether he could realistically have done anything to prevent it.

The men in Stewart's unit had fought in the Battle of Lookout Mountain (Chattanooga) in Tennessee by the spring of 1864 and had retreated with other Confederate forces into Georgia. One of their members died at Cassville, near Kingston, in April. By mid-May, the Campbell Salt Springs Guards had backtracked north to Resaca, not far south of Dalton. At least two of Stewart's military comrades died and two were wounded when Sherman attacked at Resaca on May 14. Two more members of his unit were wounded at New Hope Church just west of Kennesaw Mountain and Marietta on May 25.

On July 8, the day the mill at Sweetwater Creek was burned, Walter Stewart may have been stationed less than ten miles away at Powder Springs, where two members of his unit, James Kerley and William Mitchell, were captured. Union scout reports indicate that at least one band of Georgia State Troops was near Sweetwater around July 12. Were these men aware of the situation with the millworkers at Sweetwater Creek factory? Were they attempting to do something about it? No records exist that can positively answer those questions.

Manning Payne deserted the Campbell Salt Springs Guards at Powder Springs and was captured eight days later on July 16 in Campbell County. Payne apparently turned himself in to Federal troops in the area because, less than a month later in Louisville, Kentucky, he took the oath of allegiance to the United States government. Payne was then released with orders to cross the Ohio River and remain north of that point until the war ended.

It is impossible not to wonder what was going through Walter Stewart's mind on July 8, 1864. Did he know what was happening in Sweetwater Creek? Did he make any attempt to slip away and check on his family? Stewart was obviously a loyal Confederate soldier. Even though he told Lizzie months earlier that he felt he had been in the war long enough, he stayed with his unit and did not desert as so many others did in 1864 when the southern cause began to look hopeless.

From our distant vantage point, with so few records available, we know only that Synthia Catherine's father was not far away when her tragic journey began. While the Union Army wagons that would carry his family to Marietta lumbered toward

Sweetwater Creek, Walter Stewart and other members of the Campbell Salt Springs Guards were about to receive orders to move with a host of other Confederate troops to set up a strong defense of Atlanta.

At dawn on the morning of July 9, the high-wheeled, white-capped Union Army wagons began to appear at the meeting place on the bank of Sweetwater Creek. Synthia Catherine, her family, and all of the other families who likely camped there all night—the Humphries and the Demooneys, the Newburns and the Lees—climbed into the wagons and settled in as comfortably as they could for their journey.

S. H. Causey brought his older brother from the woods, and the two of them helped their mother find the younger children places in one of the wagons. S. H. was relieved to see Federal soldiers treating the people kindly. They were not rough with the women, and they gave everyone food. The Union forces seemed to have the attitude that the people of Sweetwater Creek were not at fault in this war, that they were only pawns forced to make cloth and uniforms for the true rebels who were hell-bent on defying their legitimate country.

Margaret White, who was at the meeting place with her two small children, possibly wondered how her husband, A. J., would ever find her if she made this journey. All the people knew was that they were headed for Marietta, where they would be transferred to railroad cars at the Western & Atlantic depot, which was under Yankee control. From there, they would travel north.

Synthia Catherine clutched her Bible, which she chose the evening before when her mother allowed each child to choose one special possession to take along on the journey. As Synthia Catherine climbed into the wagon, a Yankee soldier stopped her and snatched away the Bible. He was gone from the side of the wagon before Synthia Catherine could protest.

CHAPTER 6

TAINTED WITH TREASON

On July 1, 1864, in Roswell, the day before General Stoneman's troops rode to Sweetwater Creek and placed the New Manchester millworkers under guard, the Confederate units protecting the bridge at Roswell withdrew and headed twenty miles away to support their left flank at another point along the Chattahoochee. There were four to five hundred soldiers in the units that withdrew, and when they were gone, only the locally organized battalion of less than one hundred men remained to protect the town of Roswell.

Captain Will H. Clark, the commander, received a report on Sunday, July 3, that Confederate troops evacuated Marietta the night before. It was painfully clear that Sherman's forces were coming closer. Clark wrote to Ralph King, suggesting that King come immediately to consult with him about how to defend the town.

Almost none of the original planter family settlers remained in Roswell. Most had fled, loading up whatever possessions they could manage and transporting them across the bridge to railroad depots in Atlanta. Some of the families arranged for their slaves or employees from the mills to take care of their homes and property until they returned. Dr. Nathaniel Pratt and his family stayed in town; on July 3, the widow of Thomas E. King was apparently still living at Bulloch Hall with her three children. She rented the house from Martha Elliott Bulloch, who had left Roswell for New York City after her daughter Mittie's wedding to Theodore Roosevelt in 1853. Martha's grandson Theodore, born in 1858, became the twenty-sixth president of the United States.

Clark advised Ralph King that all of the ladies, "especially Mrs. Tom King with her children," should leave Roswell immediately. Mrs. King took Clark's advice. Before leaving she asked mill weaver

Bulloch Hall was built in 1839–40 by Major James Stephens Bulloch of Savannah. The parents of President Theodore Roosevelt were married in this house in December 1853. The widow of Thomas Edward King was living here with her three children when the Yankees approached Roswell in the summer of 1864. Mill employee Theophile Roché flew the French flag from its high portico in an attempt at feigned neutrality. *(Sketch from ROSWELL HISTORIC HOMES AND LANDMARKS by artist Ernest DeVane used with permission of the Roswell Historical Society)*

Theophile Roché to look after Bulloch Hall. He was close to her family and to the Smiths, whose children he tutored in French from time to time.

Theophile Roché, John N. Brown, and Samuel Bonfoy still worked at Ivy Woolen Mill that summer. Olney Eldridge and George Camp, chief agent for Roswell Manufacturing Company and the husband of Henry Merrell's sister, were still at work in Roswell, and so were more than three hundred others employed by the three mills. By July 1864, most of the workers fell into three categories— women whose husbands served in the Roswell Battalion and other Confederate military units, young single girls, and mill family children ages ten through early teens.

On Independence Day 1864, and exactly one year after the fall of Vicksburg, Sherman ordered the Second U.S. Cavalry Division to proceed to Roswell. When Sherman issued the order, he was not concerned about destroying a strategic southern industrial complex. His objective, as stated in his orders to Garrard, was to counteract the enemy and keep them from attacking Union communications and the Union-held Western & Atlantic Railroad.

Sherman viewed "Roswell Factory" as having great importance, but mostly because of the nearby bridge and fords that might be passable. "In case the enemy's cavalry get across [the Chattahoochee River]," he told Garrard, "you must hang to him, opposing him whenever opposition is possible, and send couriers rapidly to me, and to the points of the railroad threatened."

On Tuesday morning, July 5, Garrard's mounted division headed for Roswell from Ruff's Station (now called Smyrna), where they had been engaged in battle. Troops from Michigan, Pennsylvania, Ohio, Illinois, and Indiana rode with Garrard that day.

Women and children at the Roswell mills knew Union troops were coming. Many of their husbands, brothers, and sons served in the Roswell Battalion, and when Roswell was threatened, about eighty members of the battalion elected to stay and defend the town.

Another seventy-five officers and men formed a cavalry unit that mounted up and rode out to make a stand against the Seventeenth Indiana Mounted Infantry and the First Ohio Volunteer Cavalry. The Roswell Battalion unit met those troops near a paper mill on about two miles west of Roswell. They skirmished with the Yankees but had to fall back. While the Yankees burned the paper mill, the Confederate battalion, along with the Ninth Tennessee Cavalry of the Confederate Army, retreated to Roswell and across the Chattahoochee.

Allenbrook served as the office and home of the Ivy Woolen Mill superintendent in Roswell. *(Sketch from ROSWELL HISTORIC HOMES AND LANDMARKS by artist Ernest DeVane used with permission of the Roswell Historical Society)*

Before the battalion withdrew from Roswell, Captain James King sought out his mill superintendent, Samuel Bonfoy. Most likely, George H. Camp also attended that meeting. "Keep all this machinery running just as long as you can," King told Bonfoy. "Don't shut down unless the soldiers drive you out."

At eleven o'clock Captain Clark ordered the Roswell Battalion to leave the town behind and cross the bridge over the river. One of the last things the husbands, brothers, and sons saw as they left Roswell was Ivy Woolen Mill, the smallest and newest of the town's mills, situated at the fork where Vickery's Creek empties into the Chattahoochee. Few of their wives, sisters, and daughters worked in that mill, but the men glanced at the upper-story windows anyway, hoping to catch sight of a loving wave or two just before they entered the 600-foot-long covered bridge. Then they rode their horses through the wood-framed darkness to the other side of

the Chattahoochee, burning the bridge behind them and ful-
filling orders first issued in May through Confederate Adjutant
A. W. Harris.

It did not take long for the bridge to go up in flames because it
was padded with cotton and straw from one end to the other. It
burned fast and would not provide easy passage for Yankees pushing toward Atlanta. After crossing the bridge, men in the Roswell
Battalion looked back and saw the dark beams whoosh up in flame.
Soon, the entire structure crumbled and fell into the muddy river
waters below.

With the bridge destroyed, the best place to cross the river in
Roswell was the shallow ford near the bridge. It was as if the town
reverted to the transportation pattern of its beginnings in spite of

Barrington and Catherine King raised their nine children in Barrington Hall
after its completion around 1842. General Kenner Dudley Garrard is said to
have established his headquarters here when he occupied Roswell. *(Sketch from
ROSWELL HISTORIC HOMES AND LANDMARKS by artist Ernest DeVane
used with permission of the Roswell Historical Society)*

all its progress since then. The ford was the same one Roswell King and other founding families used to reach the site of the future Roswell when they first brought their carriages and wagons to the area.

Women and children in the cotton mills did not see the battalion enter the covered bridge or watch the burning timbers fall into the river below. As on any other day, they had worked nearly five hours by eleven o'clock. Perhaps Atlanta Lindsey had a brief chance to kiss her husband, Ransom, goodbye during the breakfast break earlier that morning. Perhaps Lavina Fretwell waved at Littleton. But when the bell sounded for lunch, the women and girls were able to step outside and smell smoke from the bridge.

Fifty-seven-year-old Private Jonathan Farr, a watchman for Roswell Manufacturing Company, was among 182 men listed on the official roster of the Roswell Battalion. When the battalion withdrew, he made the fateful decision to remain behind with his forty-six-year-old wife, Jane, and their four children. At the time of the 1860 census, his son Joel and daughter Martha worked in one of the mills, while Nancy and Amanda remained at home. Since census takers made their rounds only once every ten years, we do not know if Jonathan's son Joel or any of his daughters worked in the mill the day the main unit of the Roswell Battalion rode across the bridge and burned it.

Jonathan's twenty-eight-year-old son, Samuel, worked as an overseer for Roswell Manufacturing Company. Samuel's wife, Rebecca Jane, cared for their two-year-old son, Jonathan, who was named after his grandfather. Perhaps because he was an overseer and still exempt from mandatory service, Samuel was not a member of the Roswell Battalion and remained at his job in the mill.

Littleton B. Fretwell and Isaac Fretwell were also privates in the Roswell Battalion. Census records for 1860 suggest the two were father and son and worked as factory hands in one of the mills. Littleton Fretwell was fifty-five years old and married to Lavina, who was fifty-three.

Records also suggest that twenty-six-year-old Isaac, also called Charles, lived at home with his six younger sisters—Frances,

Martha, Jane, Nancy, Caroline, and Louisa. The Confederate War Records housed in the Georgia Department of Archives and History state that Isaac and nineteen other members of the Roswell Battalion deserted their unit on July 4, 1864, the day Garrard's troops entered town. Atlanta Lindsey's husband, Ransom, was also among that group. There is no reason stated for their desertion, and they apparently remained at large in the Roswell area almost until the end of July.

The Wood family came to Roswell around the beginning of the war, perhaps expressly for the purpose of working in a mill that needed many employees to meet its contracts with the Confederate government. Before the war, the family lived near Ringgold, Resaca, and Dalton. John and William Wood were privates in the Roswell Battalion. Their father, Robert A. Wood, fought for the Confederacy earlier in the war, but he got sick and died while home on a Christmas furlough in December 1863. In July 1864, Margarette Wood was caring for her three daughters—Lucinda Elizabeth, Mollie Ann, and Easter—as well as for her mother, Mary Ann Sumner, who lived with them. Records do not indicate which of these family members worked in the Roswell Manufacturing Company mills in 1864.

Twenty-six-year-old Third Lieutenant John R. Kendley was also a member of the Roswell Battalion, along with his sixteen-year-old brother, Thomas Hugh. Their youngest brother, fifteen-year-old George, is not listed on the battalion's roster. George was probably working in the mill the day the battalion retreated.

John R. Kendley also was not among those who rode across the bridge ahead of the Union troops. Kendley, like S. H. Causey's brother in Sweetwater Creek, had no desire to spend the rest of the war in a Federal prison camp. Because he had signed an oath not to fight when he was wounded and captured earlier in the war, Kendley left town on his own so he would not be captured again. He knew he could be shot on sight if Union soldiers found him fighting with a Confederate unit after signing the oath of allegiance. Perhaps Kendley hid out for a time in the woods, as Causey's brother hid near Sweetwater Creek, to avoid capture.

Thomas Hugh Kendley also was not with the Roswell Battalion that day. Instead he was working in the mill with George and two of his sisters, twenty-eight-year-old Sara Jane and Mary, who was about to celebrate her twenty-first birthday. Neither sister had married.

The oldest Kendley daughter, Elizabeth, may have been married by this time and may even have moved away. The same could be true of twenty-seven-year-old Catherine. Like a number of Roswell mill women, the record of their lives has not been traced beyond the events of the first week of July 1864.

General Garrard's advance guard, the Seventh Pennsylvania Cavalry, was not far behind the Roswell Battalion. But the guard arrived too late to save the bridge. When Garrard learned the bridge had been burned, he sent a courier with the information to Captain Dayton at Sherman's headquarters, along with the news that he had sent out a regiment to burn paper mills, flour mills, and machine shops in the Roswell vicinity. Sherman had already passed through Marietta, and just that morning had set up headquarters at the Pace House in Vinings.

As members of the Seventh Pennsylvania Cavalry reached the banks of the Chattahoochee, they spotted Ivy Woolen Mill in a patch of woods just east of the pilings where the bridge had spanned the river only hours before. The mill was still in full operation in spite of the Yankee intrusion. Like the mill at Sweetwater Creek, Ivy Woolen Mill had contracts with the Confederacy. Its workers furnished more than fifteen thousand yards of high-quality woolens every month for the "Roswell gray" uniforms worn by thousands of Confederate military volunteers.

Weaver Theophile Roché ran the French tricolor flag up the pole above Ivy Woolen Mill. The banner flapped in the hot, sultry breeze as the Yankee troops first cast their eyes in the direction of the mill. The broad red, white, and blue stripes of the French flag also flew above the portico of Bulloch Hall, not far from the town square.

Captain Joseph G. Vale of Company M in the Seventh Pennsylvania saw Roché and several other Roswell citizens approach Union Colonel Robert Minty. "Sirs, we are subjects of Great Britain and France, and we are under the protection of those nations." That was what Roché told the officers, no doubt in the thickest French accent he could manage. "We demand our rights as neutrals that you respect us and our workers and our property."

When he made those statements, Roché was either carrying out specific orders from the King family or had decided that the best way to preserve the mill property was to masquerade as a French national producing cloth and yarn only for export. Roché might have had well-intentioned motives, but his statements and actions spelled disaster for Sara Jane and Mary Kendley, Rebecca Jane Farr, Lavina Fretwell, and for Margarette Wood and her elderly mother. Tuccorah Moore, Sarah James, Georgiana Morgan, the Fretwell girls, the Wood girls, and others suffered because of Roché's masquerade.

Roché's claim of foreign protection was absurd, and it was probable that Union officers recognized this from the very beginning of the Frenchman's short, elegant speech. Nevertheless, the Yankees politely assured Roché that his rights and the rights of other workers would be fully accorded and respected if they were truly neutrals and were not engaged in aiding southern belligerents.

Since Minty had no direct orders regarding the textile mills, he directed Roché and the others to Garrard's headquarters on the bank of Willeo Creek not far west of town. Garrard assured the Frenchman that he had no direct orders to burn the wool and cotton mills and gave Roché and those with him passes to travel freely around the occupied town.

On Wednesday, July 6, Garrard rode into Roswell to personally inspect Ivy Woolen Mill. After he made his way down to the creek bank, Captain Vale watched him step inside the brick building. Millworkers were at their various workstations carrying out their assigned duties in the production of dense woolen cloth. Garrard began his inspection on the top floor, where the picking and packing work was done. No doubt the few girls who worked there stared with fright as the Union general with the curly beard entered their workroom.

Accompanied by the mill superintendent, Garrard descended to the carding room and to the spinning room. It was only a matter of minutes before Garrard entered the weave room and reached out to inspect the web on one of the two hundred sixteen looms. Garrard saw there, plain as day, as Captain Vale later described them, "the cabalistic letters C. S. A." woven proudly into the web.

Garrard stepped back outside the building and summoned the "neutral subjects of Great Britain and Imperial France" to explain themselves. That, of course, they were unable to do. Garrard ordered the French flags lowered at the mill and at Bulloch Hall.

"Get all the workers out of this building at once," the Union officer demanded. "You have just thirty minutes to get them all out."

When Roché refused, Union soldiers charged in to clear the premises, ordering everyone to put down their work. The millworkers filed out, some of them cowering and crying at the sight of the soldiers lined up outside gawking at them.

The mill superintendent was supposed to remove money and private papers under supervision, but several sources suggest that he refused to cooperate, prompting Union troops to seize the mill books and papers to send to their headquarters. Union officers apparently questioned Theophile Roché, power loom bosses Jason S. Wood and John N. Brown, and Theodore Adams, Barrington King's assistant. Records do not mention Samuel Bonfoy, who may not have been at the mill that fateful morning.

Evidently, George H. Camp was not on the premises either. He wrote a letter to Archibald Smith the following week, indicating that he had left Roswell just before the bridge at "Ivys Mills" was burned and the "vandals" (Union troops) entered town. Camp hurried from Roswell to Curtright, where his cousin Henry Merrell had gone when he left Roswell, and took a position with a manufacturing company there.

While soldiers evacuated Ivy Woolen Mill, Captain Darius E. Livermore of the Third Ohio Cavalry took possession of the two French flags and issued a receipt. "This will certify that the bearer Mr. Theophile Roché has voluntarily given the undersigned two French flags," the receipt said. "His property will receive the same protection as though the flags still remained on this premises."

Garrard then dispatched inspectors to check the two nearby cotton mills and sent Sherman word that his troops now occupied Roswell. Sherman replied from his headquarters near Vinings and told Garrard that "Atlanta is in plain view." He cautioned Garrard to keep his main forces concealed while he guarded the Chattahoochee and determined the best place to cross.

Colonel Abram O. Miller led a detail of the Seventy-second Indiana Mounted Infantry, including Private Silas C. Stevens of the Chicago Board of Trade Battery, to the two cotton mill buildings on the banks of Vickery's Creek. As they descended the dusty, winding road to the creek bank, Stevens saw that these mills also were humming along at full capacity as if no invasion were taking place. He heard an aide to Miller ask the proprietor to show them around the workrooms. The colonel wanted to know how the machinery worked, what kind of rebel goods were being manufactured, and how many women, girls, and children were inside the buildings.

Sara Jane and Mary Kendley were working in one of these mill buildings on July 6. So were Thomas Hugh and George Kendley. Frances, Martha, and Jane Fretwell were there too, along with John Moore and at least one of the Hopkins girls. They were among the bewildered workers who filed quietly out of the mill buildings as superintendents followed Union orders to shut down the machinery. Later, some of the millworkers remembered Union soldiers giving them cloth and provisions as they left the building. Other millworkers, however, recalled Union soldiers taking all the cloth for their army hospitals.

An eerie silence settled in when the machinery lurched to a stop. The millworkers heard only the rushing water as they stood in the dappled sunshine and whispered among themselves. Some of them cried; some were angry. Would the Yankees burn their only means of making a living? Would they leave the workers alone? Mothers gathered their children around them.

Private Stevens stared at the polished machinery that filled one building from the top story to the basement. It seemed such a wanton act to burn everything, but then he reminded himself of the old adage, "All is fair in love and war."

Someone else burned the mill building while Stevens took two men to assist him in burning the nearby storehouse. He recorded his actions in a letter home, writing that he burned the storehouse from the top down by placing cotton saturated with oil on each floor. "My idea was not to endanger the buildings of the residents of the place, whose houses were in the immediate vicinity." He reasoned there was less danger from sparks that way, because the floors of the building fell on top of each other, into the basement, and then into the waters of the stream.

Stevens seemed proud that his storehouse was completely consumed by flames before the mill fire was underway. He noted in his letter that he took great pleasure in the work.

Gradually, the Roswell Manufacturing Company employees realized they were out of work and would not be staying in Roswell. As the workers stared at the flames in disbelief, Yankee soldiers began rounding them up. "Get your things. You will not be staying here," they ordered. "Every last one of you is to come to the town square within the hour."

Under guard, the workers walked in small clusters to their homes and apartments to gather what they could. No one knew what would happen next. The Old Bricks apartment dwellings where many of them lived had been commandeered as a makeshift hospital for wounded Yankees. Blue uniforms were everywhere, swarming around the company houses and even the mansions on the other side of the square.

As they walked ahead of the Yankee soldiers, the women no doubt worried not only about what was going to happen to them, but also about their husbands and sons who crossed the Chattahoochee bridge and then burned it behind them. A few of their sons had joined Isaac Fretwell in deserting Roswell Battalion that day and were hiding nearby. It would be many months before most of those women would be able to begin tracing what happened to their husbands and sons.

Some of the young girls flirted with the Union soldiers as they climbed the dusty pathways to the center of town. They even flaunted a little lace and silk, as one officer wrote to his sister. But most of the women made venomous eye contact with the soldiers, warning them that God and the government of Jefferson Davis would punish them for burning property and arresting innocent civilians.

Mary Kendley riveted two Yankee troopers with the hatred in her eyes. "I'll remember every last one of you," she shouted. "Every one of your ugly, Lincoln-loving faces!" She stood near the edge of the square, almost unable to comprehend what was happening despite weeks of rumors. She tried to keep George and Thomas Hugh with her, but they dashed among the others, jostling for better views of the blue-coated soldiers.

"Shush!" Sara Jane cautioned her sister. "You'll get us into more trouble than we're already in."

"I'm going to look every last one of them in the eye," Mary said. "They won't make me look down in shame. I'll stare them down first. I want to remember forever what they are doing to us today."

Sara Jane shook her head. Her sister's spirit surprised and amused her.

The glaring sunshine beat down on the square, making it brutally hot. By the time the Kendley sisters arrived, other millworker families already occupied the few patches of shade. They sat down on the brittle summer grass, trying to keep their brothers in view. "They have no right," said Mary. "We're not in the Confederate Army. There are supposed to be regulations about things like this."

Samuel Farr spread a blanket in a quiet corner of the square for Rebecca Jane and their baby. She had been chased out of her apartment and was grateful to find Samuel waiting for her at the edge of the grass. Jonathan was whimpering, and Rebecca Jane rocked the baby against her to quiet him. Behind the company store, dark smoke rose from the creek gorge where the mills still burned.

Samuel and Rebecca Jane saw his parents make their way slowly up the street to the square.

Margarette Wood was one of the last to arrive at the meeting place. She pleaded with the soldiers to allow her to stay in her apartment with her elderly mother, but the soldiers insisted that everyone go to the square. Margarette spread a small quilt for her mother and eased her down on it. Then she gathered her daughters, warning them not to look up at the soldiers if they knew what was good for them.

Eighteen-year-old Lucinda Elizabeth tried to follow her mother's advice but found it difficult not to sneak quick peeks at some of the young Yankees clearly admiring girls her age who gathered in bewilderment on the square. Fifteen-year-old Mollie Ann and eleven-year-old Easter also took quick peeks at the soldiers, but they turned their eyes quickly to the ground the minute one of them looked back.

The Yankee soldiers stared at the millworkers. Some of them teased and taunted, "Making rebel uniforms, were you? We'll teach you to defy your rightful government! I'm gonna find me a Stars 'n' Stripes and make you all stand up and salute it."

Some of the soldiers seemed sympathetic. They brought water buckets and promised food. "We know this isn't your fault," they said. "You were just doing what you were told, weren't you?"

At seven o'clock that evening the ruins of textile mill buildings were smoldering. The machinery was scattered over the creek banks where it had fallen as the flooring burned out from beneath it. The air remained hot and sultry even at twilight.

Garrard had gone back to Willeo Creek and compiled a summary report for Sherman. In addition to information about geography and military encampments, he wrote, "There are some fine factories here, a woolen factory, capacity 30,000 yards a month." He listed the output of each mill and stated that a six-month supply of cotton was on hand when he arrived. "Over the woolen factory the French flag was flying, but seeing no Federal flag above it I had the Building burnt," Garrard reported. "All are burnt. The cotton factory was worked up to the time of its destruction, some 400 women being employed."

It is natural to wonder whether Garrard would have acted so quickly if the French flag had not been flying above the mill. Or if Sherman had not chided him recently for being too cautious and too slow.

Many of the occupying Yankees who camped in Roswell talked among themselves about what they had learned from "the niggers" (their words) in the town. "Those mills and the whole country around here is owned by the Kings. The Kings control the store and the provisions and everything, and they don't allow any liquor to be sold."

The soldiers also talked about the paper currency used in Roswell, currency said to be more valuable than Confederate scrip. They heard that the Kings left Roswell the night before with a wagonful of "hard money" in chests. And they heard the town used to have one thousand residents in addition to the factory girls.

The last mill fires burned themselves out about 10:30 the night of July 6. Exhausted and bewildered, the millworkers and their families tried to stretch out in the somewhat cooler night air for some sleep. Nearly three hundred people crowded together on the once-attractive town square, with Yankee patrols keeping watch around them.

Garrard may have attempted to get back into Sherman's good graces when he moved so quickly to burn the Roswell mill buildings. Sherman was obviously pleased when he responded to Garrard's report on the morning of July 7. "I assure you, spite of any little disappointment I may have expressed, I feel for you personally not only respect but affection, and wish for your unmeasured success and reputation." Not to welcome Garrard back into his favor too easily, Sherman added that he still wanted to inspire all of his cavalry leaders with his conviction "that caution and prudence should be but a small element in their characters."

Sherman indicated surprise that the factories in Roswell were still in production when Garrard arrived. He had assumed all the machinery had been removed previously by the secessionist owners. "Their utter destruction is right and meets my entire approval," declared Sherman. "And to make the matter complete you will arrest the owners and employees and send them, under guard, charged with treason to Marietta."

Like Garrard, Sherman was outraged at the conduct of Theophile Roché. "I will see as to any man in America hoisting the French flag and then devoting his labor and capital in supplying armies in open hostility to our Government and claiming the benefit of his neutral flag." Sherman gave Garrard a free hand in dealing with Roché. "Should you, under the impulse of anger, natural at contemplating such perfidy, hang the wretch, I approve the act beforehand."

Then Sherman sealed the fate of the women and children laborers of both Roswell and Sweetwater Creek. His decree would also apply to any men still working with the women and children or living with them in these towns. "I repeat my orders that you arrest all people, male and female, connected with those factories, no matter what the clamor, and let them foot it, under guard, to Marietta, whence I will send them by cars to the North." He directed Garrard to burn any other sawmills and factories in the area and treat any skilled laborers exempt from Confederate conscription as much like prisoners as if they were armed.

"The poor women will make a howl," Sherman predicted. "Let them take along their children and clothing, provided they have the means of hauling or you can spare them. We will retain them until they can reach a country where they can live in peace and security."

At eleven o'clock the morning of July 7, Sherman filed a report with Union Army Chief of Staff General Henry W. Halleck in Washington, outlining what had happened in Roswell. "I have ordered General Garrard to arrest for treason all owners and employees, foreign and native, and send them under guard to Marietta, whence I will send them North," Sherman wrote. "Being exempt from conscription, they are as much governed by the rules of war as if in the ranks. The women can find employment in Indiana."

Since the owners of the Roswell mills were not in residence and the supervisors were treated somewhat less severely, it was the employees—mostly women and children—who were arrested. When the arrest announcement was made at the square, a general moan and then an outcry went up from the workers. "How can they do this? It isn't right," said Mary Kendley.

Ivy Woolen Mill loom boss John N. Brown stated in court testimony in 1882 that he left Roswell at seven o'clock on the evening of July 7 in a wagon train furnished by the Union Army. He and a group from the mill, perhaps including Theophile Roché and other bosses, headed for Marietta. Whether this group was officially under arrest or not was never made completely clear during the court proceedings. Later many of the mill bosses testified that they left freely on their own and that the Federal troops who escorted them to Marietta were provided only for their protection.

During the early evening, a correspondent for the *Cincinnati Daily Commercial* sat on the porch of the company store, compiling an interesting bit of editorializing about the events in Roswell. His words would appear in his newspaper two weeks later, on July 20. The correspondent scribbled down the general details of the burning of the mill buildings and the orders that the female millworkers were to be sent north. Then he began to record his impressions of the economic situation in southern towns such as Roswell. His paragraphs reflected the attitude of many Yankee soldiers and war correspondents who entered Georgia in the summer of 1864.

> The wealthy lords who have domineered in this country for years, left their homes of ease and comfort and fled before the 'advancing foe.' Their homes, filled with all the luxuries of wealth, were taken possession of and their effects given to the poor over whom they had lorded for time passed forever. 'Twas a fitting disposal of their gains, and

speaks too plainly the feelings General Sherman entertains for the poor and deluded people of the South, who have had no hand in bringing upon the country this awful rebellion. It speaks to the poor who are yet in the clutches of the Confederates, in tones louder than proclamations or promises . . . In the war of the rich on the poor, the arms of the Union are offered as a protection to the downtrodden, and by this act General Sherman has called upon them to trust him and give themselves to his care.

Several reports printed later charged that the millworkers ransacked the mansions of Roswell after the wealthy owners fled town. Evelyn Barrington Simpson made such an accusation in a 1938 typescript titled, "Roswell and Those Who Built It." Simpson wrote that some of the women paraded in the streets in the fine clothes of members of the Smith, Pratt, and King families.

Anna Pratt reportedly wrote to the Smiths down in Valdosta and told them that the Yankees broke into the summer home of a prominent Savannah cotton broker and told the "factory people" to take whatever they wanted. The Smiths also heard that other residences were ransacked and that the Presbyterian church was stripped of everything, including the organ pipes.

On Friday morning, July 8, Garrard moved his main troops into Roswell, where they camped in the middle of town, many of them pitching their cramped white tents on the sloping lawns of Great Oaks while the Dr. Nathaniel Pratt and his family watched from their windows with resentment and anger. Garrard set up his own headquarters in one of the stately homes. At least one source suggests it was Barrington Hall, the home of Roswell King and his family, opposite the town square. Because portions of Wheeler's cavalry and other Confederate units could be seen clearly just on the other side of the river, Garrard ordered the Federal troops not to build campfires that night.

No campfires were allowed on the town square either. The ranks of the millworkers thinned out some, but most were still camped there, waiting to learn what was to become of them. They had heard the order that they were to be sent north. But where was that really? And what would they do when they got there?

On July 9, Sherman wrote again to Halleck in Washington. He told Halleck that the Roswell mill had been "engaged almost exclusively in manufacturing cloth for the Confederate Army," and he referred to an enclosed paper that showed the mill owners had transferred their property "to the English and French flags for safety." But Sherman concluded that kind of nonsense did not fool him. "They were tainted with treason, and such fictitious transfer was an aggravation. I will send all the owners, agents, and employees up to Indiana to get rid of them there. I take it a neutral is no better than one of our own citizens engaged in supplying a hostile army."

On the same day, Sherman sent a message to General Webster in Nashville alerting him to expect the millworkers to arrive there. In that message Sherman referred to millworkers from both Roswell and Sweetwater Creek. "When they reach Nashville have them sent across the Ohio River and turned loose to earn a living where they can't do us any harm," Sherman told Webster. "If any of the principals seem to you dangerous, you may order them imprisoned for a time. The men were exempt from conscription by reason of their skill, but the women were simply laborers that must be removed from this district."

Webster must have been puzzled when he received that directive from Sherman. It was still a long way from Nashville to the Ohio River. In order for Webster to send those people across the river, he would have to make arrangements for them to travel farther north by train, on the L & N Railroad line, to Louisville, just across the river from Jeffersonville and New Albany, Indiana.

Although John N. Brown and some of the other mill managers left Roswell for Marietta as early as July 7, the Kendley brothers and sisters, the Farrs, the Fretwells, and many others did not escape the heat and primitive conditions of the Roswell town square quite so quickly. Captain John W. Tuttle, Company G, Third Kentucky Voluntary Infantry, wrote in his diary about what he saw as he entered Roswell a day or so later: "About 400 factory girls lined the sides of the road as we passed, presenting quite a sad appearance as they were thrown out of employment and seemed not to know where they would go or what to do."

Another soldier quoted in the *Cincinnati Daily Commercial* on July 20 described Roswell as a small village on the banks of the Chattahoochie (his spelling). He said Roswell was known for its large factories and that approximately seven hundred girls were employed in them. "Most of these are now homeless, friendless, and pensionless," said the soldier. "If you could but look upon their young faces and see the appeal for sympathy written there, you would involuntarily think, 'How little the women of Northern America know of the real concomitant evils of this war.'"

A member of the Seventy-third Regiment of Illinois Infantry Volunteers wrote about his arrival in Roswell, which he described as a small manufacturing village with nice houses in shady groves that looked "decidedly inviting." He estimated the number of factory girls in the town at eight hundred and reported that many of them went that day to Marietta with the Federal supply train of wagons. The writer had the impression that the factory girls preferred going north to staying where they were.

On Saturday, July 9, Sergeant Benjamin F. Mager of the Seventy-second Indiana recorded that the bugle sounded for preaching at ten o'clock in the morning. He painted a picture of every nonassigned Yankee soldier crowding into one of the mansions to hear Chaplain DeLaMatyr conduct an especially impressive service. "Could the common people of the South have been permitted to look upon our devotions, they must have been convinced that we Yankees were not the vandals their leaders had pictured us to be," wrote Mager.

A rainstorm the night of July 9 drenched the weary Union soldiers as well as the millworkers huddled in the open on the square.

As happens in Georgia, the rain cooled the air only temporarily. When the sun came out the next morning, it combined with the moisture in the air to create a steambath effect. The captives on the square moved very little. Their clothes were sodden, and each step sucked mud up through what little grass was left. The air was so thick Mary Kendley thought she could reach out and touch it if she had cared at all to move.

Margarette Wood worried about her mother, who slept only fitfully during the night while Margarette and her daughters huddled around, trying to keep her dry.

Sergeant Mager's unit seemed to have forgotten the serious preaching by Sunday morning, July 10. His brigade camped for the first time in the middle of civilization, in the center of a southern town, and apparently quite close to the female millworkers. "There are more of them [women] than we had seen since leaving Nashville," wrote Mager.

Mager went on to describe how Garrard kept an earlier promise and sent a round of whiskey to the men on their day of rest. It was Mager's opinion that the men did not ask for whiskey, did not need it, and would have been better off without it. He described a common military habit in which each man who wanted whiskey drew his ration, but then some men gambled with each other "drink for drink" until some won enough to get gloriously drunk.

According to Mager, on this occasion the gloriously drunk members of the unit began making love to the women millworkers. Some of the girls, the ones who already had flaunted their silk and lace, seemed quite willing, to the delight of the Yankee soldiers. But Colonel Abram Miller put a quick stop to that. He moved his soldiers a mile north of town and set up a new camp.

By late Sunday afternoon the soldiers in Mager's unit had been marched away from the women. The women, along with their children and a few husbands and fathers, had all left Roswell for Marietta. Yankee military units continued to occupy Roswell and settled on the town square, the broad lawns, or in the elegant residences, depending upon their rank. The Union troops transformed Roswell's churches into makeshift hospitals.

Mary Kendley celebrated her twenty-first birthday in the back of a canvas-topped Union Army wagon as it rumbled over the bad road between Roswell and Marietta. She had no idea where she would be when she turned twenty-two. Her only consolation was that Sara Jane and her two younger brothers were with her. John Robert's wife, Susan, had not been picked up by the Yankees, and Mary prayed that she and little Julia would be all right until John Robert could make his way back safely to care for them.

One Illinois soldier wrote to his wife on July 11 that he arrived in Roswell the day before and found the millworkers still there, very short of provisions. In this soldier's version, his unit comforted and cared for the workers who were still in Roswell and then sent them to Marietta. "It was a fine sight to see 400 girls all at once, a sight we do not often see in the army," the soldier wrote.

Private Henry Orendorff of the 103rd Illinois wrote home that he expected people had seen the account of the capture of the Roswell factory. "I just wish they would issue them [the five hundred women] to us soldiers," he wrote. "I believe they sent them back to Marietta, I wish our Regt was back there on Provo Duty."

Another *Cincinnati Daily Commercial* correspondent put a particularly interesting slant on the events of that week in Roswell. His account, dated July 11, appeared on July 19 in a column titled, "Rebel Accounts." It described the arrest of the Roswell factory workers as one of the more novel arrests in the history of war.

> Giving "aid and comfort to the enemy" they [the mill-workers] most assuredly were, and much valuable tent-cloth; but in the case of many of them, it was an involuntary service, since they had been confined and compelled to labor there without cessation from the breaking out of the rebellion. Then too the cartel makes no provisions touching the exchange of prisoners of this sort; neither would it do to send them across the lines to their former employers, since they would immediately be set to the

manufacture of tents again; nor was it safe to discharge them unconditionally in the midst of two great armies, many of them far removed from their friends and helpless.

The newspaper correspondent was not clear about where he thought those girls were from or in what manner they were confined. There is no local evidence to support his impressions. Census records suggest that the young girls among the millworkers were mostly members of large families and that most of those who were not born in this part of Georgia came from other parts of the state or from North and South Carolina. Most of them, or at least older members of their families, worked in the mill well before the war began.

The correspondent went on:

Thus red tape was about to become involved in a hopeless entanglement with crinoline, tent-cloth, and cartels, when General Sherman interposed and solved the knotty question by loading them into 110 wagons, and sending them to Marietta, to be sent north of the Ohio, and set at liberty. Only think of it! Four hundred weeping and terrified Ellens, Susans and Maggies transported, in the springless and seatless army wagons, away from their lovers and brothers of the sunny South, and all for the offense of weaving tent-cloth and spinning stocking yarn!

This highly emotional account randomly picked out the names "Ellen, Susan, and Maggie" to make a point. It is interesting to note that among the women who were sent north, there may have been only one Ellen—Ellen Smith who, according to the 1860 census, would have been twenty in the summer of 1864. There were numerous Susans, including Susan Drake, who was twelve years old and the daughter of an overseer at one of the mills, and Susan Owens, age forty-three, the wife of factory hand David Owens and the mother of six girls. There were at least three

Margarets—Margaret Morgan and Margarette Wood of Roswell and Margaret White of Sweetwater Creek—who might have been called "Maggie" by their friends and families.

CHAPTER 7

EVERYONE HEADING NORTH

William Tecumseh Sherman sent General Stoneman's troops south toward Sweetwater Creek at the beginning of July 1864. Synthia Catherine Stewart, her family, and other millworkers cowered in their homes under guards posted by Major Haviland Thompkins, waiting for the Union Army wagons to arrive. Sherman ordered General Garrard to make his move toward Roswell, where he would burn the mills and arrest the workers, including the Kendley brothers and sisters and members of the Fretwell and Farr families.

Confederate General Joe Johnston gave up his fortified position at Kennesaw Mountain. He moved his troops through Marietta and ordered everything belonging to the Confederate Army to be shipped out immediately. Some of Johnston's forces tore up miles of telegraph wires, as well as the rails of the Western & Atlantic Railroad line before they retreated south. They even took the frogs from the railroad switches.

As residents of Marietta prepared to flee south, they dismantled whatever they thought might be of use to the invading Yankees. Unfortunately, those efforts caused only minor delays. Within days—and in some cases within hours—the Yankees had the telegraph and the railroad up and running again.

When the sun rose on the morning of July 3, the Federal flag was waving above Kennesaw Mountain, visible in the distance from Marietta. By 8:30 Sherman was standing in the town square, not long after General Joseph Wheeler's cavalry had left. As Sherman surveyed the town, have he might been wondering where the war had taken Arnoldus Brumby, his friend from West Point who was once in charge of Georgia Military Institute. Or perhaps he was remembering the sketches he made of Kennesaw years before when he served in an artillery unit here. Officially Sherman had been defeated at Kennesaw a few days earlier, but he was now clearly in control; Joe Johnston was on the run.

Sherman had not yet heard about the events in Roswell. He and a few other Union generals already had sent numerous southern sympathizers from the Carolinas away from their homes on charges of treason, but he had not yet ordered any cotton mill-workers to the North.

Sherman and General McPherson headquartered for the day in the hotel that later became known as the Kennesaw House, a fashionable brick building with white-trimmed pillars and balconies near the town square and the Western & Atlantic Railroad

By 8:30 a.m. on July 3, 1864, General William Tecumseh Sherman had captured Kennesaw Mountain and stood triumphantly on the square in the middle of Marietta, Georgia. He was given quarters in the Kennesaw House, a fashionable hotel near the square and the Western & Atlantic Railroad depot. Sherman had already left Marietta when the millworker families arrived on July 9. *(Photo of restored Kennesaw House by Barney Cook)*

depot. General George H. Thomas set up his headquarters for the Army of the Cumberland just up the hill from town at Georgia Military Institute.

A correspondent for the *New York Tribune* tagged along with the Union troops as they entered Marietta on Sunday morning, July 3. He declared it the finest town Federal troops had seen since crossing the Ohio River. "The streets are well laid out; the private residences are upon an ample scale, and many of them elegant. They are mostly embowered in clumps of shade trees, and the better portion of them are ornamented with flower gardens exhibiting taste and culture."

The correspondent painted a poignant scene of the invaders tramping past the churches of Marietta that Sunday morning while the few people who had not fled as refugees stood inside singing hymns. About ten o'clock people could hear the bells of the Episcopal church pealing out the call to worship.

The *Tribune* correspondent was impressed with the commanding view from "the hill"—the Georgia Military Institute grounds with fine shade trees and the "princely residence" of Colonel Arnoldus Brumby just off the parade ground. The cadets had left to serve at West Point on the Alabama border, destined to later march ahead of Sherman most of the way to Savannah. Brumby was gone too—he was fighting now instead of administrating.

The boots of curious Yankee enlisted men trampled Brumby's prized roses when they peeked in the windows of his abandoned home, and the main building of the institute was looking "seedy." Only hours before, it had functioned as a temporary hospital for wounded Confederate soldiers.

"It must have cost the citizens many a pang to tear themselves away from the grateful shade and quiet comfort of the luxurious homes of Marietta to wander in the Saharas of Southern Georgia at the present hot and dusty season," wrote the correspondent. He speculated that fewer than twenty homes were still occupied, and those only by elderly men, invalids, and children unable to travel quickly.

On Sunday afternoon regiment after regiment of Union troops marched through Marietta. One Michigan artillery officer declared the stately mansions of the town even more beautiful than the elegant residences on Michigan Avenue in Detroit. That same officer added, however, that there was "an air of desolation about the place," with most of the stores and homes empty and Union Army stragglers beginning, against express orders, to plunder the unoccupied houses.

The *Cincinnati Daily Commercial* declared that most of the one thousand inhabitants of Marietta left town either before or with the rebel army in its retreat, "leaving their deserted houses and gardens as trophies for the 'invading horse' of Lincolnites." One article suggested that, of the forty or so houses believed to be still occupied, most were inhabited by "rabid, rebel women" who rushed inside and locked their doors whenever Yankee officers approached.

Another soldier, who signed himself "Quartus" in the *Cincinnati Daily Commercial*, described Marietta as "a pretty country town, on the railroad, and about twenty miles from Atlanta." This writer said the residences were aristocratic with no expense spared. "Its hotel is a grand affair, and the Military Academy there boasts of having had many honored pupils in the South. The people are disloyal of course but 'very tired of the war' since it bodes them 'so much evil and so little good.' "

On Monday, July 4, General Thomas ordered the town garrisoned as a military post, with a brigade of the Fourteenth Corps to remain until July 13. Thomas reminded his troops that they should "endeavor to preserve public and private property in Marietta as nearly as possible in the state in which you found it, and to prevent plundering and pillaging." His orders directed that no officer was to take quarters in Marietta without Sherman's approval and that any "Union people desiring to go north for the purpose of remaining there" should receive transportation for themselves, their families, and their baggage.

Thomas also directed that "all resident rebels" be arrested and that all cotton that had been abandoned or that belonged to the rebel government be turned over to the quartermaster's department for shipment north. Some of this cotton may have belonged to the King family, the Smith family, or to other Roswell Manufacturing Company stockholders.

On this Independence Day, as the summer heat began to rise during the morning hours, the Union troops subjected the remaining residents of Marietta to lively, patriotic band music and enthusiastic cheering.

People came to Marietta for a variety of reasons. Sweetwater Creek mill founder Charles McDonald chose to live there after he retired as governor of Georgia. William John Russell maintained a residence in Marietta while he supervised work at Sweetwater Creek. S. H. Causey and other young Sweetwater Creek millworkers traveled to the town by wagon in 1862, when they expected to be mustered into the Confederate military. And one of the Sweetwater Creek supply wagons was traveling to Marietta when desperate women seized it and stole its load of fabric in 1863. Marietta had long been a storage depot for incoming unprocessed cotton as well as outgoing finished cotton textiles and yarn from both milltowns.

During the second week of July 1864, all the millworkers from Sweetwater Creek and Roswell were brought to Marietta in Union Army wagons because of the railroad lines, which Sherman was rapidly reconnecting. He was determined to keep his supply route opened through Chattanooga and Nashville to Louisville. He was also determined to remove, wherever possible, any unfriendly populations that could close in behind his army as he advanced through Georgia. In the case of Sweetwater Creek and Roswell, this meant mass banishment.

Some of the Roswell millworkers arrived in Marietta the morning of July 9, after a sixteen-mile wagon ride over bad roads during the night. Mounted units from Garrard's forces escorted this group. Just as they had done outside the mills and on the town square in Roswell, the millworker families riding in the wagons had to endure the stares of a new batch of Union soldiers who were both puzzled and amazed at their situation. Considering where the people in the wagons had spent the past few days and nights, they most certainly appeared bedraggled. Their hair was stringy, their calico dresses and bonnets stained and mussed, and their eyes blank or filled with fear and frustration.

An obviously Union-biased correspondent for the *Louisville Daily Journal* who watched the wagons bring millworkers into town wrote, "It was really a sad spectacle to witness these young women, accompanied by their parents and smaller brothers and sisters, come into Marietta to get transportation to the land of plenty beyond the confines of the so-called Southern Confederacy." He went on to elaborate, "The deep anguish of soul experienced by thousands and tens of thousands of human beings, who were happy prior to the outbreak of the rebellion, should cause the mad fanatics who inaugurated the war under the false plea of ameliorating their condition, to take the second sober thought, and abandon their unequal warfare against the best government in the world."

When the wagons reached the Georgia Military Institute grounds up on the hill, a provost guard from Colonel Newell Gleason's Second Brigade relieved Garrard's men and ushered the captives into the abandoned classrooms. Union troops were quartered in the more comfortable ten-man barracks that lined the institute's parade ground.

Major General Grenville M. Dodge, who came in from the field to visit wounded soldiers, looked with pity at the many young, frightened girls. Private James P. Snell of the Illinois Infantry wrote in his diary that Dodge ordered the chief surgeon to hire as many of these girls as he could as nurses for the sick and wounded. They were to be paid and given rations, as allowed by Union Army regulations. Mary and Sara Jane Kendley were not among those the surgeon hired. Neither were Rebecca Jane Farr and Margaret Morgan. But some of the mill girls stayed in Marietta when the trains pulled out for Louisville.

The next day, a second wagon train rolled through the streets of Marietta bringing the men, women, and children from

Sweetwater Creek. Synthia Catherine Stewart was riding in one of those wagons, staring out at the town's wide streets. They must have looked very different from the much more primitive village scenes of Sweetwater Creek. She saw the blue-coated Yankees lining the main street as the wagon bumped along. She also saw the grand, white-trimmed Fletcher House hotel, where the Union officers were in residence, along with Denmead's Warehouse and the railroad depot.

Synthia Catherine's eyes swept the clusters of Yankee soldiers, wondering which of them her father might have fought recently. Months had passed since she and her mother had heard from Walter. He could be anywhere, but he promised he'd come home if the Yankees reached Atlanta, and Marietta was near Atlanta. Synthia Catherine prayed her father was on his way to help them.

She continued to study the rugged faces of the Yankee soldiers. Had any of them been in Vicksburg, where she was sure her father had fought? Had any of them been at Sweetwater Creek just a few days ago? Suddenly, her eyes fixed on one particular face. "There he is, Mama!" she cried out. "There's the one who took my Bible!" Her sharp eyes spotted something distinctive about one of the enlisted men.

Before Lizzie Stewart could stop her, Synthia Catherine stood up in the wagon, pointing her finger and yelling. "That's the Yankee devil who stole my Bible! Somebody grab him and get my Bible back!"

The Yankee soldier looked up in surprise and turned to walk away from the wagons, but it was too late. Synthia Catherine made so much fuss that she drew the attention of a Union officer riding with the wagon train. "Stop right there!" he ordered the enlisted man.

As Synthia Catherine told the story to her grandson years later in Texas, it was Sherman himself who stopped the thief and returned her Bible. Probably it was another high-ranking Union officer who took the time to help this angry nine-year-old. But no matter who it was, *some* Yankee returned Synthia Catherine's Bible to her, and it remained in her possession for the rest of her life.

Garrard's superior, General George H. Thomas, learned that millworker families arrived in Marietta and sent his own dispatch to Sherman, who had left Marietta for Vinings. "The Roswell factory hands, 400 or 500 in number, have arrived in Marietta," he wrote. "The most of them are women. I can only order them transportation to Nashville where it seems hard to turn them adrift. What had best be done with them?"

Sherman was not concerned with sentiments about setting civilians adrift. "I have ordered General Webster in Nashville to dispose of them," he replied. "They will be sent to Indiana."

Barrington King's brother William was in Marietta on July 10. William King was a successful cotton factor and commission merchant from Savannah who, for some reason due to business or family background, considered William Tecumseh Sherman a personal friend. Later in the summer King attempted to negotiate a meeting between Georgia Governor Joseph E. Brown and Sherman in an effort to end the war; but on July 10, his concerns were not that broad. King recorded in his diary that he walked over to the military institute and talked with Olney Eldridge and Samuel Bonfoy, who were held there. "The factories in Roswell have been utterly destroyed," Eldridge and Bonfoy told King. "We have all been arrested, even the operatives [millworkers], and now we're on our way north."

Eldridge and Bonfoy also told King that the houses of all the planter families in Roswell were broken into and plundered. "Everything of value has either been taken away or destroyed, and the operatives [millworkers] did most of it. Not the soldiers."

Disappointed by this news, King wrote, "What a comment on the human character." He went on to record that he had been under Yankee occupation in Marietta for one week and stated that he had not found the northerners particularly disagreeable. "And greatly to my surprise, even among the common soldiers with whom I have also conversed freely, I have seen exhibited no exultant spirit expressed at our army having so constantly fallen back; but more a spirit of sympathy, for us, and simply a desire to avoid any expression which may be painful to me." King wrote that the Yankees who spoke with him did not appear to feel any hatred toward southerners. Rather, he wrote, they "speak favorably of our army and our people, they say we are one people, the same language, habits and religion, and ought to be one people, they have a higher opinion of the people in the South than before the war."

King's conciliatory attitude got him into trouble later in the summer with many of the Roswell planter families because they viewed his attempts to set up conversations between Sherman and Brown as a misrepresentation of Georgia's support for the Confederacy. In fact, they accused King of telling Sherman that Georgia would be willing to withdraw from the Confederacy to gain protection, which in their view, was far from the truth.

When Synthia Catherine Stewart and others arrived in Marietta from Sweetwater Creek, the buildings of the Georgia Military Institute were already packed with rebel prisoners, including the Roswell workers. The Sweetwater Creek millworkers and their families were expected to camp outside.

A great number of northern women— some of them married to Union officers in the garrison—had already arrived in Marietta. Synthia Catherine watched as a group of northern women ventured onto the military institute campus one afternoon to look at the southern women. Lizzie Stewart, Amanda Humphries, and others sat with their children in the shade of a huge tabernacle on the parade ground between rows of barracks.

The northern ladies stood off to themselves for a while, just looking and whispering. But eventually they stepped into the shade of the tabernacle and began to ask questions. Perhaps they were looking for souvenirs to take home from their sojourn in the South.

"What kind of goods is that dress made of?" one of them asked Amanda Humphries. The woman smiled as Amanda looked down at her dress in surprise. Amanda wondered why anyone would care about the disheveled thing she was wearing. She had made the dress a few years earlier from cloth Lizzie Stewart had woven for her on the loom in the Stewart farmhouse.

"It's homespun," Amanda told the woman, who looked back at her with puzzlement. "You know, homemade cloth. It's woven at home, on a hand loom."

"I'd like to have that dress," said the woman.

Amanda laughed. "Well, I don't see how you can," she answered, glancing about the open tent surroundings. The other Sweetwater Creek women laughed with her. A couple of them sang a few lines of a familiar tune:

> *My homespun dress is plain, I know,*
> *My hat's quite common, too,*
> *But that will show what the Southern girls*
> *For the Southern boys will do.*
> *Hooray, hurrah, for the sunny SOUTH, hurrah,*
> *Three cheers for the homespun dress,*
> *That the Southern ladies wear.*

The tune made the dress even more appealing to the northern woman. "I really want to buy your dress," she said. "We're about the same size. I'll pay you well for it." As the other northern and southern women giggled and shook their heads at this exchange, Amanda and the woman made their way into one of the buildings and exchanged dresses. The woman paid Amanda what she considered a fair sum and then wandered off with her friends. Synthia Catherine never told her grandson what Amanda Humphries wore after that day—whether it was the northern lady's dress or another she had in a bundle with her.

On Wednesday, July 13, Theodore F. Upson was part of the 100th Indiana Volunteer Infantry unit assigned to guard the Roswell workers. "We have some 400 young women in the old Seminary building near town," he recorded later. "They have been working in a factory at Roswell making cloth for the Confederate government. The factories were destroyed and the girls are to be sent south or north whichever way they want to go. Some of them are tough, and it's a hard job to keep them straight and to keep the men away from them."

Upson noted that even Sherman recognized the difficulties. "General Sherman says he would rather try to guard the whole Confederate Army, and I guess he is right about that."

On Thursday, July 14, William King visited the mill employees again. It was raining when he headed for the grounds of the institute, but he continued on anyway. "I saw several of the Roswell factory operatives [millworkers]," he wrote. He mentioned that Mr. Wood was among those who were on their way "to the North." This was Jason S. Wood, a power loom boss from Roswell Manufacturing Company.

The first reports of trainloads of millworkers and other refugees leaving Marietta for Nashville appeared in northern newspapers on July 15. A *New York Tribune* reporter wrote on that date that "one or two trainloads" of the millworkers had been sent north.

Two days later, another newspaper article announced, "The refugees from the Sweetwater Factory and from Roswell are going north by train as fast as transportation can be afforded. The Union Army has issued each person nine days' rations for the journey."

Major Haviland Thompkins, of General Stoneman's staff, was in charge of looking after the comfort of the millworkers held in Marietta. Thompkins also had been in charge of burning the mill in Sweetwater Creek and arresting the operatives there. It was he who oversaw the issue of military rations as the disheveled workers climbed aboard the railroad cars at the Western & Atlantic Railroad depot.

On July 15, 1864, at least two trainloads of Sweetwater Creek and Roswell millworkers and their families traveled north from Marietta to Chattanooga, Tennessee, where they could see Lookout Mountain rising behind the railroad depot. For more than a year, Chattanooga had served as a Union base. *(Photo of railroad yard and depot in Chattanooga taken in 1864 or 1865 courtesy of the Library of Congress, Prints & Photographs Division, reproduction number LC-B8171-2655)*

As the long journey north began that July morning, Synthia Catherine held tight to the flat bench she sat on in the smelly railroad car. A small homespun bag slung across her shoulder held the Bible that was returned to her. Although the railroad car was fitted with benches and a window or two, her nose told her that the car was recently used to transport animals. It most likely had also transported Yankee soldiers.

Synthia Catherine held her little sister Linnie's hand tightly to keep her from tumbling onto the swaying, straw-covered floor. Her older sister Sarah watched out for little Jim, while Lizzie and Uncle James sat by themselves, whispering grownup worries so the children wouldn't hear. A blue-coated Yankee soldier rode silently along with the millworkers in each car.

It was hard to leave little Jeff's grave there all by itself in Sweetwater Creek. Synthia Catherine and Linnie decorated it carefully with sprigs of ivy and a tin of wildflowers the afternoon before leaving their farm. It was also hard to leave the only place Papa would know to look for them. "We'll write him as soon as we know where we will be," Mama had promised, but Synthia Catherine knew the truth. Mama had no idea where to write to Papa.

Lizzie managed to bring a small sack of food for the family to supplement the Union Army rations. All together "in a little old wad about as big as your two fists," she carried pickled pork, a little syrup, some beans, some crackers, and a treasured loaf of bread.

Mrs. Causey rode on the same train. She was so happy to have her two oldest sons and her smallest children with her. She knew that no matter what happened, they would handle it better if they were together.

Amanda Humphries rode north too, perhaps thinking about her homespun dress and why on earth that northern woman found it so appealing. Would all the women up north put stock in such things? She gathered her littlest ones around her. Mary, who was eight, would view all this turmoil as an adventure, but poor little Eugenia was probably bewildered. Amanda wondered what happened to her son, John, and Lizzie's husband, Walter. She knew they fought at Vicksburg, because they came home on leave afterward, but there had been no news in a long while. The Mozley boys were with them in the Campbell Salt Springs Guards unit.

The Sweetwater Creek people stayed together, but they knew millworkers from Roswell were heading north with them. They heard that they would all travel first through Chattanooga and then on to Nashville. Specific orders about their future went only that far, and as the journey began, they considered the hopeful possibility that they would be freed in Nashville, which was considerably closer to home than the other side of the Ohio River. But

Union soldiers also told them that Sherman's orders were to ship them all the way to Indiana, on the northern side of the Ohio River.

Later that day, Private William Miller was on duty at a railroad siding in Kingston, Georgia, northwest of Marietta along the Western & Atlantic route through Dalton, Georgia, and Chattanooga. "We passed a large train loaded with refugees or citizens going north to where they can live until the war is over," he wrote. "They are a poor ignorant set."

By July 15, at least two trainloads of Sweetwater Creek and Roswell refugees had chugged north out of Marietta along Sherman's newly restored railroad tracks, which ran through Cartersville, Kingston, Adairsville, and Resaca. Those towns already bore the thumbprints of Union Army destruction and occupation even though Sherman's final desecration of Georgia would not begin until fall.

The railroad cars were pulled by steam engines that hissed and whooshed each time the trains sped up or slowed down. The steam was generated by coal—dirty, sooty stuff that stuck to clothes and sweaty faces, especially in mid-July. The women were grateful whenever the train sped up on a straight stretch of track because that created a breeze and freshened the air in their cars.

The grade was steep at times in the foothills of the Appalachians. The train had to climb through Ringgold Gap and burrow through Tunnel Hill.

It must have been frightening to children like Synthia Catherine and her sisters to see for themselves the burned-out houses and shredded farmland of this countryside where battles had scarred the landscape. A solitary chimney mourned here and there for a home and family that once clustered around it.

One of the young boys in Synthia Catherine's car had heard someone in Marietta telling about how the Yankees cured

Confederate guerrillas of planting torpedoes on the railroad tracks. "They were hiding 'em wherever the Yankees were fixing the tracks for themselves," the boy excitedly told little Jim. "One of the guards in Marietta told us all about it. General Sherman would get his men to round up the important secesh sympathizers and make 'em climb into an old boxcar, and then he'd pull that boxcar along the track. If it didn't go boom! and explode all the Confederates, he knew it was safe for his soldiers to ride on that stretch. It didn't take long for the Georgia guerrillas to stop hiding torpedoes on the tracks when they heard he was doing that."

Synthia Catherine's eyes widened as she listened to the story. She hoped the track ahead of them didn't have any torpedoes. She peeked at the Yankee guard riding in their car. He pretended not to hear what the boy was saying, but she could see him smiling.

In Dalton, their train track merged with others as they veered west toward Chattanooga. Uncle James had heard in Marietta about how the Yankees stole a steam engine on this railroad line two years earlier. While their own train swayed on the same tracks, Uncle James entertained the children by telling them how the Yankees commandeered the *General,* running it toward Chattanooga to destroy the Western & Atlantic track. The engineer, his conductor, and his machine foreman chased after them on a push car and on another steam engine. Their bravery checked the Federal troops for a while, but not long enough.

Lookout Mountain rose in the background as the train pulled into the Chattanooga station. The railroad had been in Chattanooga nearly fifteen years. For more than a year, the city had served as a Union base for Sherman and other Federal generals. It provided a vital link in Sherman's chain back to his supplies in Louisville, to where he was sending all the people from Georgia.

Peering from the few windows in the railroad cars, the Georgia refugees saw that mountains almost entirely surrounded Chattanooga. The sloping hillside beyond the one-story, tin-roofed depot was dotted with row upon row of white canvas army tents. The Yankee tents were like the ones on the military institute grounds in Marietta, but there were many more of them on the hillside.

Chattanooga was perhaps a fitting first stop for the Roswell and Sweetwater Creek people on their way north. Twenty-five years earlier, the Cherokee had begun their westward trek from the same city. Sad names echoed from the surrounding countryside—Lookout Mountain, Signal Mountain, Missionary Ridge, and Chickamauga. This had been a bloody, bloody place.

Synthia Catherine sampled a dry biscuit from the rations Yankees gave them. Lizzie reached into the sack she brought and handed her daughter a chunk of bread. "This won't keep forever," she said. "Enjoy it now while it's still almost fresh."

From Chattanooga the trains continued to Nashville, which was roughly the same distance as from Atlanta to Chattanooga. Nashville had been under Federal control for two years when millworkers arrived, and it would be another five months before General John Bell Hood would make a last-ditch effort to snatch it back from the Yankees in mid-December.

When the car Synthia Catherine and her family occupied reached the rail yard, they saw switching tracks veering off in several directions. The brick depot had two stories, and its windows had painted shutters. Everywhere they looked, the millworkers saw trains huffing and puffing. Every few minutes, they heard mournful whistles, announcing an arrival or departure of solemn, blue-coated soldiers or displaced people such as themselves.

Union soldiers hurried the captives off the trains as soon as they arrived on July 19 or 20. No one has verified the exact date for any specific group of refugees, partly because Nashville was such a busy place in 1864.

Guards walked down the streets with Synthia Catherine and others to a military prison set up near the depot. People along the way stared at the millworker families without saying a word.

Union soldiers served a quick meal at the prison. Someone handed Synthia Catherine a smelly piece of beef liver with a crust

Mill refugees spent the night of July 19 or 20 in Nashville, Tennessee, on their way north. The city had been occupied by Federal troops for two years. *(Photo of railroad depot in Nashville as it appeared in 1864 courtesy of the Library of Congress, Prints & Photographs Division, reproduction number LC-B8171-2651)*

of bread, and even though she was hungry, her stomach churned. "Don't put that in your mouth!" Lizzie whispered. "Just hold it so they'll think you're grateful. I'll slip you a little pickled pork as soon as they move on."

Synthia Catherine nodded in agreement. She wandered the courtyard, listening to snatches of one conversation and another. Not everyone milling around was from Sweetwater Creek. At least one hundred other tired-looking people milled around in bunches, some eating the food passed out by the soldiers. From a distance, Synthia Catherine watched her mother pull a small tin from her dress pocket and give it to Sarah so she could get water for each member of the family from the big barrel.

The Sweetwater Creek refugees spent that night in Nashville. Toward evening, a reporter from the *Nashville Daily Times* moved among the small clusters of people. He asked questions and scribbled furiously on a little pad of paper. He had heard about the trainloads of women and children from Marietta. "About 200 of them," his editor told him. "Go on down there and see what you can find out."

What the reporter learned from the Sweetwater Creek people, we already know. He learned that the millworkers were making yarn and osnaburg for the Confederate Army. And he found out that the men on the train were mostly exempt from the army because of their skills or their inability to fight due to illness, like Uncle James with his rheumatism. Sherman ordered all of them sent north of the Ohio River to earn a living where they would be unable to help the Confederacy.

Much of what the reporter wrote about Sweetwater Creek millworkers was speculation. Some of it seems based on conversations with people whose pride encouraged them to put a rosy light on their situation. He wrote that, as a group, the millworkers fared better than many other classes of people in the South. The reporter also wrote that the workers earned about six dollars a day for their labor, which had been in great demand. He said they were well protected by the Confederate government and were shielded from conscription because of their skills. All of these statements were exaggerated. "If they are honest, well-disposed people," the reporter concluded with optimism, "they can readily find employment at excellent wages."

Perhaps Synthia Catherine wandered outside that night in Nashville and stood a moment or two looking up at the stars twinkling peacefully in the darkness, high above all the confusion. She didn't see any falling stars, but remembered her father's words so long ago on the bank of Sweetwater Creek. That night on the creek bank, her father told millworkers the North would war against the

South to free the Negroes because the North wanted to break up the way things were done in the South.

The North had certainly broken things up, Synthia Catherine probably thought to herself. They freed the Negroes in every southern district they invaded, but arrested the millworkers. It was all so confusing. Somehow it was ending up all wrong.

In another of the trains headed north, Sara Jane and Mary Kendley rode with their younger brothers, Thomas Hugh and George. Records from 1864 are scarce, so we do not know if their sisters, Elizabeth and Catherine, began the journey with them.

Samuel and Rebecca Jane Farr were on a train too, cuddling tiny Jonathan. They worried about leaving behind Samuel's parents, Jonathan and Jane, and Samuel's younger brothers and sisters. Again the records are scarce, and we do not know if other members of the Farr family journeyed north with them.

Other Roswell families also traveled north with no idea of what the journey held in store. All women in the Fretwell family were on one of the trains, probably with Lavina's husband, Littleton Fretwell. Lavina's six daughters were with her, but she most likely had no idea where Isaac and other Roswell Battalion deserters were when she left Roswell and Marietta.

The Moores also traveled north from Roswell and Marietta. Lively (Elirly, in some spellings) was in her early forties. Her daughters Nancy and Tuccorah, ages sixteen and twelve, and her son Robert traveled with her. Lively Moore's older son, John, was a member of the Roswell Battalion. The records do not make it clear whether he made the trip to Indiana with his mother and the rest of the family or joined them later.

Margarette Sumner Wood's family was also on a train. Margarette had a cough, probably a result of the wet night she had spent on the square in Roswell. Her oldest daughter, Lucinda, took care of her grandmother, Mary Ann Sumner, and her sisters, Mollie Ann and Easter. Researcher Michael Hitt has a family letter that suggests John and William Wood may have made this trip with the rest of the family, but there is no proof of this. John and William were members of the Roswell Battalion, but it is unclear whether they were with the women of the family in Roswell when the Yankees arrived or whether they rode across the bridge with Captain King.

Some people not arrested by Federal troops were allowed to make the trip on their own by taking Union trains to Louisville, Indianapolis, or other places north of the Ohio River. They were not under guard once they reached Marietta. Some of them held higher positions within the Roswell mills, and a few apparently agreed to take an oath of allegiance to the United States to gain freedom of choice about their future. Those people had some money and property, unlike the general millworkers, or "lintheads," who were mostly penniless even before the journey.

John and Mary Brown were among this slightly more elite group from Roswell. They climbed aboard the first Union Army wagon that headed for Marietta on July 7, after Yankees burned the mills. The French weaver Theophile Roché was with them in the wagon, along with mill superintendent Olney Eldridge, his daughters, and the family of Theodore Dwight Adams, a thirty-five-year-old, New York-born assistant to Barrington King at one of the mill factories.

John and Mary Brown were heading for Indianapolis, and when their train pulled in at a station somewhere between Chattanooga and Nashville, they were able to leave the train and stroll around on their own before traveling on. Mrs. Brown spotted Theophile Roché walking by himself and carrying an old valise she recognized as the one he had carried when he first arrived in Roswell several years earlier. "I'm continuing on to Nashville or maybe Cincinnati," the French weaver told her. "Maybe I can find some kind of work there." Later she reported that she and her husband never saw Roché again.

Theodore Adams' wife, Ellen, was very sick when the Yankees arrived in Roswell. He put her on the train in Marietta, hoping she could reach her family in New York while he looked for work with a Confederate munitions concern in Augusta. Ellen died in Cincinnati on August 12, and Theodore remained in the South.

The George Hull Camp family also fit into the "slightly more elite" category in Roswell. They worked for a living and ranked somewhere between the wealthy planter families and the general millworkers. Camp served as Barrington King's chief agent of Roswell Manufacturing Company after Henry Merrell left. He was also from Utica, New York, but strongly supported the Confederacy during the war. His first wife was Henry Merrell's sister, Lucretia. After Lucretia died in childbirth at the Archibald Smith home in Roswell, Camp married Jane Atwood.

George and Jane Camp packed their trunk sometime before Yankees arrived and burned the Roswell mill buildings. They arranged to ship some of Archibald Smith's family furniture, including a beloved piano, and left Roswell just before the retreating Confederates burned the bridge by Ivy Woolen Mill. On July 15 Barrington King wrote to tell the Smiths that George Camp and his family had left for Curtwright, Georgia, where he had family.

As July 1864 progressed, the Roswell and Sweetwater Creek refugees blended into a steady stream of southern sympathizers transported north. Various accounts say some refugees went to live with family members in the North. Others took steamboats upriver and got off at the pier in Cairo, Illinois. Many more were simply deposited on the Indiana side of the Ohio River in towns such as Jeffersonville and New Albany. The vast majority, including the Roswell and Sweetwater Creek mill employees, passed through or remained in Louisville, Kentucky.

The *Confederate Union* newspaper printed in Milledgeville, Georgia, on July 23 reprinted an article that appeared in the *New York Commercial Advertiser* about the sad plight of the millworkers.

But it is hardly conceivable that an officer bearing a United States commission of Major General should have so far forgotten the commonest dictates of decency and humanity, [Christianity apart] as to drive 400 penniless girls hundreds of miles away from their homes and friends to seek their livelihood amid strange and hostile people. We repeat our earnest hope that further information may redeem the name of General Sherman and our own from the frightful disgrace which this story as it now comes to us must else conflict upon one and the other.

PART III
SCATTERED LIKE DUST AND LEAVES

CHAPTER 8

A FRIGHTFUL DISGRACE

By mid-July newspapers reported southern refugees arriving in various northern locations. On July 18, a Kentucky newspaper announced the arrival in Louisville of twenty-four women and children arrested by Sherman. These people, the announcement suggested, were to be sent downriver to New Orleans and out of the country.

On the following day, the New Albany, Indiana, *Daily Ledger* reported that nearly one hundred southern refugees arrived in Evansville, Indiana, in "deplorable and destitute condition." The *Evansville Times* assured its readers that humane residents of Evansville were caring for the refugees. Neither newspaper account indicated that the refugees included women and children from Roswell or Sweetwater Creek.

By Thursday, July 21, the Louisville newspapers included accounts about the arrival of some of the millworkers by train the evening before. At least 219 came into the city on the evening of July 20, and the *Louisville Daily Journal* declared them all "ardent admirers of Jeff Davis and the Southern cause."

It is not difficult to picture Mary and Sara Jane Kendley described like that. Mary Kendley was still determined to look every Yankee straight in the eye and declare her true allegiance to the Confederacy. At the depot she overheard one soldier telling another that at least a thousand more "of these secesh people" were still back in Nashville awaiting trains. "Indiana's beginning to burst at the seams," he said, shaking his head. "And no one in this motley, disloyal group will add anything good to that state."

The depot in downtown Louisville stood bleak and gray where the tracks came into town. Its windows were too sooty to peek

Portion of first passenger station, constructed in 1856, by the L&NRRCo. located at corner 9th & Broadway, Louisville, Ky.

The long railroad journey from Georgia ended at this railroad depot in Louisville, Kentucky, around July 21. The passenger depot, located at Ninth Street and Broadway, was constructed by the L&N Railroad Company in 1856. *(Only known photo of the original L&N depot used with permission of the University Archives & Records Center at the University of Louisville)*

through, and the millworkers were not allowed to step inside. Mary Kendley quickly reached for the shoulders of her younger brothers, who were not so young anymore. "You two look as small as possible," she whispered. "I don't want them separating us. Scrunch down now, you hear me?" She was greatly relieved when no one tried to direct the boys away from their sisters.

It was almost dark when Union soldiers marched the exhausted millworkers across the street to a two-story, wood-frame building. Synthia Catherine hesitated when she saw the high wooden fence. "Everybody inside now. Hurry up!" a soldier growled when she stopped to stare. The fence was all the way around the building, and several guards stood at this one gate. "We really, truly are their prisoners," she whispered to her sister. Sarah nodded, and

Synthia Catherine saw tears glistening in the corners of Sarah's eyes. They held hands tightly.

Lizzie carried Linnie Isabella, and Uncle James held little Jim's hand. Since Synthia Catherine made no more mention of her grandmother after the family left Sweetwater Creek, we do not know if Elizabeth Webb Russell was with her daughter Lizzie and the rest of the family.

That first evening in Louisville, Synthia Catherine and her family mingled with others from Sweetwater Creek and from Roswell for only a short time because everyone was very tired. Gas jets lit the long hallways of the building, but it was still too dark to see clearly. The families walked the hallways only long enough to find a somewhat private corner of a room where they could huddle and sleep. By that time they were used to sleeping with only the quilts they had with them. No one offered them pallets.

The soldiers made it clear during the train ride to Louisville that those willing to sign an oath of allegiance to the United States would be allowed to hire themselves out in Kentucky or go on to Indiana and find work there. Those who refused would remain in prison in Louisville.

The building did not smell good. It had large, high-ceilinged rooms, but they were already crowded with clusters of frustrated families and young girls who had made the journey alone. Lucinda Wood was trying her best to keep Mollie Ann and Easter from getting upset. "It will be better in the morning, I'm sure," she told them. "It only seems bad because it's so dark and we haven't seen this place in the daylight."

The soldiers carried Lucinda's grandmother in and placed her gently on a pallet in the corner. They helped Margarette hobble in too. Her cough was much worse, and she was barely able to stand up. "I'm so sorry, Miss, but there is not another pallet for your mother," one of the soldiers told Lucinda. "We're supposed to have more, but they haven't come. There's just so many of you people arriving all at once." One of them brought a water bucket with a dipper and a clean cloth.

Lucinda wished for her father. If only he were alive, he would have kept them from this terrible journey. And now she did not even have William and John with her. They were taken to the military prison across the street. She heard that her brothers would be sent to a Union military prison on the other side of the river because they had served in the Roswell Battalion. Lucinda wanted to cry, but she also wanted to stay strong for her sisters. She leaned against the wall and stared at the flickering shadows from the gaslights high up on the hallway wall. She could hear the train whistles at the L&N depot across the street.

For several days, northern newspapers wallowed in all sorts of perspectives about the plight of the southern millworkers. Most of the journalists depicted the workers as all young and female, laboring against their will for a southern Confederacy that exploited them. Some said Sherman was angry at the poor young women for their treason, while others painted him as a shining-armored knight who rescued them from certain doom in the South.

The *Louisville Daily Journal* criticized *The New York Commercial* and other Eastern newspapers for expressing shame about Sherman's actions in sending all the factory girls to the North. The Louisville newspaper suggested the easterners had the facts wrong. These unfortunate millworkers were thrown out of employment by the chances of war in an impoverished country. Everything of value was taken from them for support of the rebel army. They were not able to find food and begged Sherman to send them where they could find work and security.

Another correspondent for the Louisville paper painted an image of frightened young girls clinging to Union Army officers and begging to be removed from the desolation of the South. He depicted Sherman exercising his "generous spirit of humanity" and giving in to their begging.

This certainly conflicted with the description written by a reporter for the *Elk Horn Independent* who visited the Louisville refuge prison on July 24 to see the millworkers for himself. The reporter arrived at the prison and received permission from the attending surgeon to wander through the entire establishment. He expected to find people who were sympathetic to the Union and grateful to be rescued by Sherman's troops. "If they are a fair specimen of Georgia refugees," he wrote after his arrival, "I say let the refugees remain in Dixie. Among the whole crowd I found but two Union persons."

This reporter also was not impressed with the appearance and attitudes of the Roswell and Sweetwater Creek people. "A more degraded, ignorant, scaley [sic] set of men, women and children I never saw. Were they less arrogant and brazen-faced, I should pity them, and in fact went with the intention of pitying the poor, suffering Union refugees, but my sympathy soon sank below zero, and disgust assumed its place."

The reporter did not think the millworker refugees were happy with their situation. He reported that they called Sherman "a wolf, a bar [bear], a beast" and promised that their government [the Confederacy] would teach him suffering when they found him. He wrote that this was just a sample of their loud and bitter curses against Sherman. He also wrote that it was his understanding that the male millworkers would be sent north of the Ohio River, while the women and children would be sent to various places in Louisville to work.

Back in Roswell, the twenty men who deserted the Roswell Battalion on July 4 turned themselves in to Union troops still stationed in town. We do not have a record of their thinking, but they had apparently decided there was no longer a reason to keep fighting. Among them was Lavina and Littleton Fretwell's son Isaac.

Like the millworkers a few weeks earlier, these men were sent to Marietta and put aboard trains. They traveled under armed guard to Chattanooga and on to the Union military prison in Louisville. The prison was directly across the street from the building where the refugee millworkers, including the Fretwells, were kept. Their total journey to Louisville took about three days—from July 28 to July 31.

In their various wartime sanctuaries farther south in Georgia, the planter families of Roswell heard more reports about what happened to their town and to the millworkers they employed. They heard rumors that the mills and all of their houses were burned. They heard that Theodore Adams' wife and small children went north with the Eldredges, and that the Pratts managed to coexist with the Yankees still camped on their lawns in Roswell.

At the beginning of August, just outside the city of Atlanta, Walter Stewart was serving picket duty along with James W. Mauldin, Edward Sims, John H. Smith, and James S. Mozley. Like Stewart, Mauldin and Mozley had family members who were working in the mill at Sweetwater Creek when the Yankees arrived. These men prepared for defensive combat against Sherman's forces, and most likely they had not yet heard what happened at the mill.

Edward Sims was restless for several days. "I never really wanted to fight this war in the first place," he told Walter Stewart as they patrolled during the dark night hours. "I only enlisted with y'all because they'd have got me with conscription if I hadn't. And now there's this amnesty deal. I've a good mind to take advantage of it. They're going to win, Walter. That's all there is to it."

Walter said nothing. It did no good to argue with Sims about honor or duty.

"The South is finished anyway. What difference does it make?" asked Sims.

Walter listened but continued to say nothing.

"If I slipped off, would you report me right away?" Sims asked in a whisper. He stopped walking and stared directly into Walter's eyes. "Would you? Or would you give me time to try to find a Yankee patrol?"

"You do what you have to do," Walter answered. "And I'll do what I have to, but I won't report you."

Within minutes, Sims shouldered his small pack and disappeared into the darkness.

An hour or so later, a Federal patrol surrounded the four men still on picket duty. Walter Stewart, James Mauldin, James Mozley, and John Smith were captured and sent behind the Union lines just west of Atlanta. They saw no sign of Edward Sims. All four men refused to accept the Union offer to take an oath of allegiance to the United States, and this sealed their fate. They were ordered to spend the rest of the war in a Union prison camp.

Reports of conditions at refugee detention centers in Louisville that August and September conflicted as much as newspaper reports about refugee sentiments. One possible reason is that the people from Roswell and Sweetwater Creek may have stayed in one of several Louisville locations. In 1864 the L&N Railroad depot faced the south side of Broadway between Ninth and Tenth Streets. On the north side of Broadway, between Tenth and Eleventh Streets, stood the Union military receiving depot and barracks where refugees might have spent the first few days and nights. It is also possible that the millworker men remained in these barracks.

Directly across from this prison depot and barracks, on the south side of Broadway between Tenth and Eleventh Streets, was a refugee home and women's prison constructed just before the millworkers arrived. A second "female prison," a house at the southeast corner of Broadway and Thirteenth Street, opened in early August to provide more room for women and children. Authorities seized the house specifically to shelter refugees.

The grandmother of a woman from Woodstock, Georgia, remembered staying in a cavernous, stench-filled building. The building was probably the first female prison, directly across from the military barracks and the train depot. Her father, who was already sick, was afraid his daughters would die of disease if they stayed in such a place, and he begged Union guards to let the family find work in the town. Permission was granted, but that would most likely have required the oath of allegiance. The daughters were able to work and supported their father until all of them could return to Georgia at the end of the war.

Measles was one of the diseases that spread through the detention center, affecting at least twenty of the refugees. A measles sufferer who later wrote about her experiences described sleeping on a bare floor with no bedding.

An editorial in the *Louisville Daily Journal* on August 11 claimed not to "overdraw the picture" when it described southern refugees "huddled together in barracks provided for that purpose" and old men, women, and children "crowded together with few provisions made for comfort." It depicted people with sad, pale faces who were weary with weeping, haggard with want, and dependent on strangers.

While pleading with the public to contribute clothing, clean linen, delicacies, and cheering words, this article spoke also of sickness, death, and crude, hasty graves. "Let the philanthropic people of Louisville visit the barracks of the refugees in our city, and there behold the sorrow, destitution, and suffering presented," it concluded. "If they will but make the visit, it will require no appeal from us to arouse them to a sense of Christian duty. The need is pressing; the case is urgent; the suffering is great; and the relief in some shape must be speedily obtained . . . We hope that, for the honor of our city, some relief may be afforded to the suffering refugees. Let the ladies interest themselves in the cause of humanity."

By contrast, the editor of the *Louisville Daily Journal* visited an airy, pleasant prison building surrounded by a high enclosure. Most likely this was the house authorities commandeered and opened in early August. The editor's article first appeared in early September and was widely reprinted in other northern newspapers.

The newspaper editor described first-floor apartments with three or four double beds in each room. He saw women of all ages sewing in these rooms and similar ones upstairs as children played at their feet on the floor. Some of the women were neatly dressed and cheerful, while others wandered about with gloomy attitudes in "robes gathered negligently about them."

His article described conversations with some of the women, and it is natural to wonder if any of their names matched those of the millworkers. Could the woman with the laughing child upon her knee have been Lizzie Stewart holding Linnie Isabella? Did she tell the editor about her sunny farm home in a faraway land? She was proud that her husband and the father of her children was a soldier in the rebel army. Or was this woman Margaret White, whose husband wrote to her from Savannah two years earlier?

There was a matron with silver hair who wore a neat white cap and told of kissing her son goodbye when he went off to fight for the rebel cause. Perhaps that was Margarette Wood's mother, the elderly Mary Ann Sumner, or Lizzie Stewart's mother, Elizabeth Webb Russell.

A young girl told the newspaper editor how she whispered parting words of love under a starlit sky, and how she was proud that her sweetheart was a war-worn veteran of the Confederacy. Possibly, she was one of the Fretwell girls, or Sarah James, who was eighteen that summer.

The editor described two rooms in the back of the house where feeble, sickly people stretched out on beds. One of these was a woman "in the prime of life" who suffered great pain—possibly Margarette Wood, who had not been well since the night she spent in the rain on Roswell's square.

The editor wrote that the prisoners had the full run of the grounds around the house, which was shaded by ornamental and fruit trees. They ate army rations prepared in a way that made them "palatable" for delicate stomachs.

He concluded his article by saying that the Union cause would not have been hurt much if these people had been allowed to remain in their homes in the South.

Very few of them possess that deep intellect culture, and high social position, which exert a strong influence, and make a dangerous enemy. If they were returned to their homes today, our cause would suffer but little thereby. The sundering of them from their homes, transporting them under guard to the banks of the Ohio, and confining them in a prison here, was an undertaking more costly than it is likely to be productive of good. If they are retained in confinement, Government will have to clothe as well as feed them for they are left in a position which renders them unable to procure any means by which they can replenish their scanty wardrobes.

The local citizens of Louisville grew concerned as well. They worried about overcrowding in the prisons and about shelter, medical attention, and food for the people released. Louisville was a conquered and occupied town, and it is clear from a late-August editorial that the *Louisville Daily Journal* favored the Union point of view. In an editorial titled, "Aid for Refugees," the newspaper expressed concern about the "distress, destitution, and suffering" of the unfortunate southerners brought to their town. It placed blame for these people's refugee status squarely on the shoulders of the Confederacy, suggesting that millworkers were compelled to leave Georgia to save their lives. The article also said rebel army deserters were "ruthlessly conscripted" into the Confederate Army against their will.

Louisville formed a commission to aid refugees, and this group reported more than one thousand such people in the vicinity of the city. Nearly two hundred lived in a refugee house at the corner of Broadway and Tenth Street (the female prison mentioned earlier), and another hundred stayed at a refugee home on Broadway and Seventeenth Street. There were also many southerners scattered in the woods around New Albany and Jeffersonville, Indiana, on the other side of the Ohio River.

The newspaper editorial suggested that the refugees living in the woods might be supporting themselves by their own labor, but that as winter came on they would flock back to the city for help. "It is our duty to provide for these now and, by a little timely aid, prevent an accumulation of evils that will close in the winter months be ten times more difficult to remove." The editorial mentioned that some ladies from the city were doing what they could, and that the surgeon from the prison occasionally visited the women and children prisoners.

"There are children of every age, some so attenuated as to be living skeletons, perishing for want of proper care. Men, women, and children, of whom a vast majority are women and children, all lie together—dozens of families—in one room, and many utterly destitute." The newspaper editorial pleaded for funds to provide emergency aid for these people and also for funds to help transport them to other places where they could find permanent employment.

Synthia Catherine's family remained within the prison compound, where they had food to eat and a bed to share. Lizzie kept things as clean and pleasant as she could, but Synthia Catherine did not like spending every hour of the day and night inside a high fence. She heard the train whistles, but she could not see what was going on outside the dusty yard. In daylight hours she played with Linnie Isabella, little Jim, and other children under the trees, but she always felt the fence defying her. It constantly reminded her that the whole world was on the other side.

Ladies from town came through the gate on Sundays, bringing sweet cakes and stockings. But they never stayed long. They smiled sadly, but they didn't talk much. Everyone else who came in was a member of the Yankee Army or one of their employees.

To Synthia Catherine's great disappointment, her older sister Sarah had nothing to do with her. Sarah would turn twelve in September, and Synthia Catherine would only be ten in October. Sarah decided not to be a child anymore. She sat with the women and begged Lizzie to teach her how to sew. She stood for hours in front of the window in their upstairs room, staring into space and humming little snatches of tunes from home.

One afternoon in mid-August, Synthia Catherine was playing out in the courtyard with her younger brother and sister when Union guards allowed Uncle James to come over and visit. He had befriended some of the Union guards by listening to their stories. Uncle James told the children a tale he heard about young Abe Lincoln and how he was arrested for taking two men out in a scow to meet a passing steamboat. "The ferryman took him to court for operating without a license," said Uncle James, "but the court didn't fine him, because he'd only taken the men to the middle of the river and not all the way across."

Every time Uncle James came into the courtyard, the children begged him to take them for a walk outside on the street. "Now hush about that," he told them. "You know these Yankees won't allow you out of here. It's against their orders. Even though they know me now, they still march me over here with guns on their shoulders and make a big show of unlocking and locking that gate—as if I'm likely to do them or anybody else any harm."

On this afternoon, however, Synthia Catherine heard a bass drum beating somewhere up the street; then a horn tooting a melody joined the drum beat. It was the first music she had heard in weeks, and all the children in the courtyard stopped playing to listen. A little pipe added a second melody, and then the whole thing became a marching song. The music started to come closer, then turned away. "Uncle James, we have to go out and see that band march by!" Synthia Catherine begged. "You know the guards. Tell them we won't run away. Tell them to let you take us out to the corner. Please, please?"

"Hush now!" said Uncle James. "You know they won't let me do that."

But Linnie Isabella and Jim began to beg too. And then the other children. "Please, please! We want to see the band."

Finally Uncle James gave in and talked to the guard at the gate. "I'll stay right with them. Just right out here on the corner. They're parading prisoners through the streets for a block or two before they lock them up, aren't they?"

The guard nodded. "Yeah, the sergeant just unloaded a bunch of rebels brought up from Atlanta on the noon train. They'll march 'em down around to Maple Street and then right back to the barracks, but you know I can't let these children out there, Mr. Stewart. That's against regulations. I stretch regulations enough already to let you come over here every afternoon or so."

"But look, sir, these kids are cooped day and night. They're getting more restless every day. They have to do something besides run around the trees. I'll stay right with them and bring them back in as soon as the parade goes back by."

The guard rolled his eyes—Uncle James was hard to refuse. "All right, all right," he said. "But you make 'em all hold hands, and nobody steps one foot out into Broadway, you hear me?"

"Yes, sir," said Uncle James with a smile.

The guard unlocked the gate. Fourteen children formed a hand-linked chain under Uncle James' direction and moved out to form a row along the street. Soon the band—three men dressed in blue wool uniforms—rounded the corner from Maple Street. The bass drum beat a slow rhythm, and the tinny music of the horn and pipe danced on top of the beat. The music floated up Thirteenth Street toward Broadway. Behind the band marched two sergeants with guns on their shoulders. Behind them was a straggling cluster of a dozen or so men in ragged gray pants and stained shirts followed by two more Yankee soldiers.

The prisoners marched up the street barefoot, and Synthia Catherine stared first at their feet. Those poor, poor men, she thought. Did the Yankees steal their boots? Then as the sad parade came closer, Synthia Catherine raised her eyes and looked into the haggard, bearded face of the first prisoner behind the sergeant. "Papa?" she called out questioningly. The man just stared straight ahead as he plodded one foot in front of the other. "Papa?" she called again. She wasn't sure with all the dirt and that long, scraggly beard, but those looked like her father's narrow-set eyes, and that's the way his hair went—straight across to the side like that.

"Uncle James! That's Papa there, the very first one. We thought sure he was dead, and there he is."

Uncle James looked up. "No, Honey, it couldn't be."

Synthia Catherine stomped her foot. "Yes it is, it's Papa. I just know it is. Please go tell those soldiers that's my papa, and I want to see him."

Uncle James tightened his grip on Synthia Catherine's hand and shook his head. "Now, now, Synthia, you just be glad you got to come out here for a little bit. Don't cause me any more trouble now."

Uncle James was squeezing her hand way too tightly, but Synthia Catherine didn't say anything. She could see that he was looking hard at the man who marched by. He ought to recognize his own brother even as bad as he looks right now, she thought. If that was really Papa, Uncle James would find out when he went back across the street. And then everything would be all right.

The other children heard none of this, and Synthia Catherine was glad. If she was right, they would find out soon enough. If not, they wouldn't be disappointed.

After the band and the prisoners disappeared up the street, Uncle James marched the children back inside the fence. He stooped down and gripped Synthia Catherine's shoulders. "Don't say a word about this, young lady, but you just might be right. Let me go and see what I can find out."

Synthia Catherine had never felt so important. Her first instinct was to rush upstairs and tell Sarah what she had seen. But Mama would be there too. What if Synthia Catherine was wrong? She would raise Mama's hopes all up, and then they would be dashed to pieces. Best thing to do was wait, she decided, but that was so hard. The other children went inside to tell their mothers about how they stepped outside the fence to see the parade.

Synthia Catherine settled herself on the small patch of grass beneath an elm tree, fixing her stare on the gate in the fence around the house. Her heart pounded every time the gate opened. The first few times only soldiers and cooks walked through to deliver rations. She looked up at the house and saw Sarah staring as usual out the open window of their room. I know something you don't know, thought Synthia Catherine to herself. And if I'm right, she thought, it's the best secret anyone ever had to hold onto.

Much later in the afternoon the gate opened again, and Synthia Catherine saw Uncle James walk through it. He held a small piece of paper in his hand and spoke quietly to the guards. They nodded, and one of them walked toward the front door of the house.

Synthia Catherine jumped up and ran to her uncle. "It is Papa, isn't it?" she asked excitedly.

Uncle James nodded, smiling down at his niece. "It certainly is, and if it weren't for your sharp eyes, we'd all have missed him. He got captured in Atlanta, he says, but he's not wounded or anything. That guard's gone to get your Mama. They're going to let her have a pass to see him for just a little bit. You give them a little time now.

"Go get Linnie and Jim. Sarah's coming out to wait with you, and in a little bit I'll take you over to the barracks yard. You won't have long. That sergeant is stretching things for us, but you will get to see your papa," promised Uncle James.

Synthia Catherine felt a thrill of pride when she saw her mother dash out of the house, holding her skirts above the ankles of her shoes as she followed the guard down the steps and out the gate. Sarah crossed the courtyard to where Synthia Catherine waited with Linnie and Jim. "I was the one who recognized him," Synthia Catherine said to Sarah.

"Hmm," said Sarah, looking toward the sky. "Oh, it's just so romantic. Mama and Papa together again. I wish I could see their faces when they meet over there. Mama was sure he was dead, and Papa probably thought we all were too."

When the children were finally allowed to walk the two blocks up the street with Uncle James and the ever-present guards, they found their parents standing teary-eyed and hand in hand just outside the Union prison barracks. Walter Stewart had been able to wash his face and comb his long hair, but he still wore the same ragged pants and shirt, and his feet were still bare. The hugs and kisses and laughter of the family did not last long enough.

Walter told the children they had grown, and he thrilled Sarah by noticing what a young lady she was turning into. There was sadness telling about little Jeff, and Synthia Catherine managed to ask about his promise. "We thought you'd be back for us, Papa, but you stayed in the war."

Walter knelt down in front of his second daughter. "Sometimes," he said slowly and with sadness, "promises are mighty hard to keep—even when we want to and especially in times like these. I wanted to come. And I want to take you away from here now too but . . . "

He was interrupted by a Union guard who stepped up close. "I'm real sorry, Sergeant Stewart. This is all the time I can give you. I've stretched things all I can. You say goodbye now so I can get you back inside with the others."

"I'll come back for all of you just as soon as I can," Walter said with his last hugs. Synthia Catherine hoped this was true. She knew long months would pass before she would see her papa again. In the morning the rebel prisoners were to be marched down to the river. A steam packet would take them up the Ohio River to Cincinnati, where they would be cramped into railroad cars for the rest of the journey to Columbus and a place called Camp Chase.

CHAPTER 9

OHIO RIVER WATERSHED

During the last year of the war, William Tecumseh Sherman regarded the Ohio River as a watershed in his struggle to subdue the Confederacy. He determined to uproot everyone who supported the southern cause and relocate them north of the Ohio. Once that was done, he would not have to worry about southern civilian support for the Confederate Army or about sabotage against his own army. He could more easily rampage through the South and wrench it to defeat.

Sherman was convinced there was a ready labor market on the north shore of the Ohio River that waited to welcome rebel millworkers such as the Farr family and the Kendley brothers and sisters. Word of numerous available jobs circulated among the refugees Sherman sent north. The news convinced the Causeys, Bryan(t)s, Fretwells, Kendleys, and Moores to take the oath of allegiance in Louisville and seek transportation across the river. The Ohio was wide and relatively smooth in Louisville. But there was no bridge, and refugee millworkers had to cross by steam packet or ferry. At places farther downriver, the ferry probably was little more than a sturdy rowboat.

Not everyone in the Union approved of Sherman's policy to relocate rebel civilians. Andrew Johnson, military governor of Tennessee, wrote to a Federal officer in Georgia that he thought secessionist sympathizers were being sent in the wrong direction. Johnson's idea was to push them south along with rebel forces instead of sending them to prisons in Louisville and feeding them. Andrew Johnson later became vice president of the United States in the spring of 1865, and became president when Lincoln was assassinated in April.

Johnson, who was born in the South but loyal to the Union, believed that sending secessionists to Union-held Kentucky simply strengthened the cause of the Copperheads, or northern residents who sympathized with the South. By 1864 the Copperheads called for peace at any price. They were particularly active in border states such as Indiana and Illinois, where good trade relationships made it difficult for northerners to view southerners as enemies.

Residents of Perry County, Indiana, directly across the Ohio River from Hawesville, Kentucky, had actually passed resolutions back in 1861 stating that the river should never become a boundary between the contending northern and southern nations. In spite of the war, interests of the two states were tightly intertwined, and Perry County residents valued their friendships and business relationships with their Kentucky neighbors. They argued that any declared border should be drawn above Perry County. But their

The Ohio River is wide and calm where it flows past the Indiana Cotton Mills facility in Cannelton, Indiana. In 1865, there was no bridge, and crossings from Hawesville, Kentucky, were made by ferry. Steam packets also provided transportation between Kentucky and southern Indiana. *(Photo of the river as it appears today by Barney Cook)*

efforts failed, and the Ohio River came to define the line between North and South until Kentucky became a Union-occupied state. During the final year of the war, Sherman mentioned the Ohio River in most of his orders directing deportation of southern civilians who supported the Confederacy.

Andrew Johnson suggested that the Federal officer in Georgia to whom he wrote pass along his opinion against deportation to Sherman. The officer replied, saying he agreed the civilian rebels should be sent south rather than north, but that he had already given Sherman his opinion on this during several conversations. Sherman told the officer, however, that he was not in favor of sending traitorous civilians through his own lines under a flag of truce to relocate them farther south.

One New York newspaper stated Sherman's ability as a military commander sometimes seemed close to imbecility with regard to civilian matters. The newspaper article accused Sherman of writing "stupendously foolish orders on things political"and declared him "incapable of administering a village on practical principle."

Another newspaper talked about the silliness of "sending the ladies back and forth." This article referred to Sherman sending helpless Georgia mill girls to the North while General William Starke Rosecrans, who was in Missouri, shipped female Confederate sympathizers back to the South.

As the fall of 1864 approached, Provost Marshal Captain Stephen E. Jones—who had responsibility for rebel prisoners in Kentucky—wrote to Sherman and complained that the large number of refugees and released southern military prisoners were causing problems along the Indiana border. Jones was frustrated because his orders only allowed him to release these people on the northern bank of the Ohio, creating tremendous overcrowding in Jeffersonville and New Albany. Perhaps Jones read the *New Albany Daily Ledger* editorial expressing indignation that Indiana should be saddled with "such people."

Contrary to Sherman's assumptions of a ready labor market in towns and cities north of the Ohio River, the number of displaced southerners in Indiana greatly exceeded the available jobs—at least

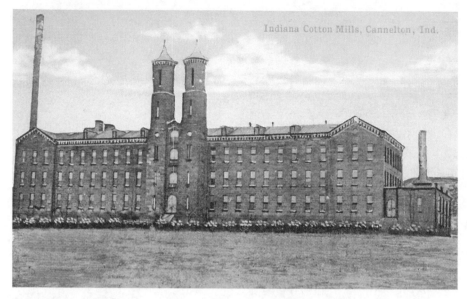

Indiana Cotton Mills, Cannelton, Ind.

The Indiana Cotton Mills facility in Cannelton, Indiana, had been in operation since 1851. It stood just three hundred yards from the Ohio River, one hundred twenty miles downriver from Louisville, in Perry County. After several shutdowns near the end of the war, the Cannelton mill returned to full blast in early May 1865 and provided jobs to a number of displaced Georgia millworkers. *(Tinted postcard view of the Cannelton mill as it most likely appeared in 1865)*

in the textile industry. The 1860 manufacturing census suggests Indiana had fewer than than eighty wool-related businesses and only two cotton businesses. These businesses were not necessarily mills and may not have been within walking distance of the Ohio River across from Louisville. With the war in progress, it is unlikely that any new mills were built in the years following the 1860 census.

Sherman might have assumed the Indiana Cotton Mills facility would need Roswell or Sweetwater Creek workers. But the mill was one hundred twenty miles downriver from Louisville in Cannelton, which was in Perry County, Indiana. The Cannelton mill had been operating since 1851 and stood only three hundred yards from the northern bank of the Ohio River.

People who built the mill thought Cannelton an ideal site because its riverfront location provided a direct water link to southern cottonfields by way of the Mississippi and Ohio Rivers. Ironically, the founders envisioned their mill as a unique experiment in North/South cooperation. They proposed that Mississippi and Louisiana cotton planters be allowed to have their cotton processed on shares. That way, the planters could own the resulting cloth and speculate on the market with fabric rather than baled cotton.

Plenty of cheap coal near Cannelton provided a ready source of fuel for the boilers feeding steam power to the mill. The town also offered an abundance of lumber, brick, and sandstone—resources that led to the development of several other industries before the Civil War.

In spite of Sherman's assumptions about the labor market, it is doubtful that the Indiana Cotton Mills company was actively seeking new employees for its Cannelton mill in the late summer of 1864, when Sweetwater Creek and Roswell workers and their families considered crossing the Ohio River. The company no longer received inexpensive shipments of cotton from southern planters after the start of the war. The company also experienced at least one work stoppage during the first months after refugee millworkers arrived in Louisville.

One of the work stoppages occurred in October 1864, and local newspapers voiced concerns about "a few hundred women and children" out of employment. Like the Sweetwater Creek and Roswell millworkers, the Cannelton employees had little education or training. Many were immigrants from Germany, England, and Ireland. And it is possible some did not know how to speak English. "This suspension will throw many persons out of employment who are unfitted to earn a comfortable living at any other occupation," complained the *Cannelton Reporter*. "It is hoped that the present stagnation in all the channels of business will shortly be removed, and our country may once more be rid of the civil commotion which is now shaking it to its foundation."

The workforce in Cannelton was largely composed of immigrants recruited specifically for jobs in the mill. At the end of a work stoppage, these former employees expected their jobs back before the hire of any new workers.

The women upriver from Louisville in Cincinnati, formed a Refugee Relief Commission that met each Tuesday to organize what help they could for those who came to their city. Newspaper advertisements from this period suggest that domestic jobs were available in Cincinnati for refugees who could afford to travel there. An advertisement in the July 30 issue of the *Cincinnati Daily Commercial* addressed "all strangers who are arriving in our city." The ad suggested women apply at the Commercial Employment Office for jobs as cooks, chambermaids, store clerks, and hotel housekeepers. A similar advertisement on August 4 sought young ladies with a genteel appearance who were good dancers and singers. The advertisement also called for canvassers, milliners, and nurses. It suggested that all strangers arriving in the city and seeking employment register at the Commercial Employment Office.

Mistaken beliefs about job availability certainly accounted for some newspaper reports about the destitute conditions of southerners forced north with little else but the clothes on their backs. Making matters worse for refugees in Louisville, the city government issued a general order on August 16, 1864, banning any rebel or disloyal person from selling goods, merchandise, or groceries. In addition, Louisville business owners were ordered not to employ rebels as clerks and were told to discharge any already in their employ by August 20.

The majority of millworkers were already penniless or close to it when they arrived in Louisville and crossed the Ohio River into Indiana. Few had the means to purchase rail or steam passages to places where they could find work. When Captain Jones wrote to General Sherman in the fall of 1864, he wanted authorization to use U.S. government funds for transporting the refugees farther away from Louisville. One of the destinations he had in mind apparently was Indianapolis, more than one hundred miles north of the river.

Sherman responded to Captain Jones' request by ordering male and female Confederate refugees, as well as deserters from the Confederate Army, transported at government expense either by steam packet to cities such as Cincinnati or St. Louis or by railroad to other points where they would have opportunities to support themselves. Sherman also ordered commanding officers at Louisville and at Cairo, Illinois, to work with Christian commission and labor agencies to help these people find honest employment.

The *New Albany Daily Ledger* expressed its approval of Sherman's new order. "Hitherto, it has been the practice to land these people on the Indiana shore without means or subsistence, leaving them to shift for themselves," reported one of the newspaper articles. "By sending them into the interior, they will better be able to procure employment and earn a livelihood, and the border counties will be relieved of a superabundance of this class of persons."

In the fall of 1864, S. H. Causey's mother remembered what she had said back in Sweetwater Creek in early July: "As long as we can earn a livelihood, we won't starve." With that thought still in mind, she and her family decided to cross the Ohio River and look for work in Indiana. Amanda Humphries decided to go too, but Margaret White, who had two small children, chose to remain in Louisville with Lizzie Stewart and her family.

Lavina Fretwell worried about what to do. Her son Isaac had been sent to a military prison camp, perhaps in Indiana. If she and her daughters crossed the river they might find him more easily when the war ended. But if she stayed in Louisville he would know where to find her. Eventually she chose to try her luck at finding work in Indianapolis.

Samuel and Rebecca Jane Farr made the same decision. Twenty-eight-year-old Samuel, formerly an overseer for Roswell Manufacturing Company, worried about the future for his two-year-old son, Jonathan. Samuel believed that with his experience he would find work in Indiana and decided it was better to take his family there than to wait in the Louisville prison for circumstances to change.

The Kendley brothers and sisters, the Moores, and the Pleas-ant Bryan(t) family also crossed the Ohio River to Indiana. No records exist to tell us exactly when those people left Louisville or if any of them left together. We only know that once they signed the oath of allegiance to the U.S. government, their papers were processed and they were released.

One particularly rainy day in the fall of 1864, Samuel and Rebecca Jane Farr climbed into a Union Army wagon with little Jonathan along with some of the other Georgia millworkers and their children. The U.S. government had agreed to transport them by army wagon to a ferry landing and pay their passage across the Ohio River. Perhaps the government also had agreed to furnish them railroad passes to Indianapolis.

Under a heavy sky that dismal, damp morning, the army wagon made only slow progress on the deeply rutted road that led to the Ohio River. It had been raining for several days, and their wagon was not the first to ply that road since the rains began. Each turn of the high, wood-spoked wheels required extraordi-nary effort on the part of the mules. At times the wagon would skid a little and sloshed at an angle. Other times it would sink into the muck almost to its axles.

This Union Army wagon was not covered by a white bonnet like the one that transported the family back in Georgia. Samuel obtained a large piece of oil cloth to shelter his wife and son, but Jonathan was restless. He didn't like being covered up and squirmed in Rebecca Jane's lap as huge raindrops pelted the stiff covering over their heads. Samuel reached in and took the boy in his arms, whispering soothing words into his ear. "It's all right, Jonathan. This rain will stop soon, and then we can watch the sun laugh at us."

The little boy looked up questioningly, and Rebecca Jane smiled at how well Samuel handled him. Jonathan was quieter already. She smoothed her damp, thick skirts and twisted the golden band that circled one finger of her left hand. "Don't worry," Samuel prom-ised. "You keep that ring no matter what."

Earlier that morning Rebecca Jane had told Samuel it would be okay if he had to sell the ring to provide for them while he looked for work. They still had the few U.S. coins for which they had traded before they left Roswell, but those wouldn't last long since they had to buy food and pay for shelter. Samuel shook his head. "We'll be fine," he said. "Don't worry about your ring."

The rain did not let up, and it got wetter and wetter in the wagon. When Jonathan began to fuss again, Samuel started to hand him back to Rebecca Jane, but the wagon lurched forward out of a rut. Samuel stumbled, and the baby slipped from his wet fingers a second too soon. Samuel and Rebecca Jane were never certain exactly how it happened, but suddenly Jonathan flew over the edge of the wagon and fell sprawling into the mud below. Rebecca Jane screamed for the driver to stop as Samuel leaped to the edge of the wagon and down to the ground.

To his horror he saw Jonathan's tiny legs kicking and flailing to the side of the wagon wheel. The baby's head and body were buried in the muck. Samuel dug frantically just as one rear wheel rolled forward over his son's head. One of the other men ran to the driver. "Pull up a little! Quick! Make those mules pull up. The Farr baby just fell out, and you stopped this thing right over his head!"

As the wagon strained forward, Samuel knelt in the mud and lifted his tiny son from the wheel rut. All the passengers climbed down, held their breath, and stood behind Samuel. Rebecca Jane was afraid to look but forced herself to watch as her husband raised the mud-covered baby in his arms. Jonathan was not moving. "Oh, my poor baby!" she cried, rushing forward. She grabbed the child and hoisted her skirt to wipe his face. Another woman, perhaps Lavina Fretwell or Elizabeth James, pulled off her shawl and ran to dip it into a muddy puddle. She handed the wet shawl to Rebecca who wiped it gently across Jonathan's face as Samuel looked on helplessly.

Samuel was sure Jonathan was dead—he wasn't struggling at all, and his arms dangled lifelessly at his sides. But when Rebecca Jane stuck her finger inside her baby's mouth and scooped out the mud, Jonathan's eyes snapped open and widened as he took in the crowd staring at him. Then, with a huge, bubbly choke, he began to scream and cry and struggle as hard as he could. Everyone present was greatly relieved. "Oh, my poor baby!" Rebecca Jane said again. She hugged him to her and handed him to Samuel so she could sit down by the side of the road and cry.

"Well, would you have believed that?" said the woman who had offered her shawl. "The Lord was lookin' out for this child when he sent these rains we've all been moanin' about. Just enough mud to cushion his precious head under that wagon wheel."

Descendants of Lucinda Elizabeth Wood and her family told researcher Michael Hitt that the Wood family was sent to Louisville, but that they made the journey by steamboat up the Mississippi and Ohio Rivers in 1863 or 1864. They heard stories about this event for years without realizing their family members were actually arrested by Union soldiers.

We know the Wood family was in Roswell when Sherman's soldiers burned the mills, and it is much more likely that the family made the journey to Louisville by train rather than steamboat. Then perhaps they embarked *from* Louisville by steamboat for Cincinnati or possibly St. Louis after Sherman's order that the U.S. government provide transportation for the refugees to other locations.

No known records suggest any other Roswell residents were sent west to the Mississippi River and upriver by steamboat to Louisville. Some references indicate that General Rosecrans, not General Sherman, ordered refugees from other areas in the South to be put ashore in Cairo, Illinois; Evansville, Indiana; and other river towns. Existing records also mention that some southern sympathizers, not Roswell millworkers, traveled by steamboat up the Tennessee River from Loudon, Tennessee, to Chattanooga before making the rest of their journey north by railroad.

Whichever way the Wood family made their journey north, descendants always heard that Margarette Wood died as she was carried in a chair by two men. It is quite possible that Margarette was in poor health, as many Roswell refugees were when they arrived in Louisville. If so, she possibly died in a chair as she was carried from the refugee prison to the pier so she could board a steam packet to cross the Ohio River. Margarette's elderly mother, Mary Ann (Polly) Sumner, reportedly died on a steamboat before it reached its destination.

Margarette's daughters, Lucinda Elizabeth, Mollie Ann, and Easter, traveled with her and their grandmother. After the two women died, the three daughters apparently returned to Louisville. We do not know if they returned to the refugee prison or, like Lizzie Stewart, found their own lodgings and managed on their own. We do know that the population of the Louisville refugee prison gradually declined beginning in September 1864 as more southerners swore allegiance to the U.S. government.

Once these prisoners gained their freedom, they had to find some means to support themselves in spite of the war or depend on kind northerners for food and shelter. Articles ran in Louisville newspapers during this time describing the extremely difficult conditions many of the released refugees faced. The southerners who left the refugee prisons no longer received army rations or shelter, and if they could not find work, they had to depend on charity. These conditions became even more difficult as the golden warmth of September and October faded to the damp, opaque cold of November and December in the Ohio River towns. It is troubling to picture the Kendley brothers and sisters, the Fretwells, Moores, and other families crowded together in tiny rooms or camping out in the woods after their release from prison.

Cincinnati and Louisville newspapers frequently mentioned refugee relief organizations that collected food and clothing to help the homeless southerners. These organizations also solicited money for medical care and transportation to other places. We know that some of the Roswell and Sweetwater Creek millworkers and their families made it as far north as Indianapolis. But they still were not guaranteed instant employment and creature comforts. Most of them struggled to meet their most basic daily needs.

One evening in late 1864 a group of Roswell millworkers were abandoned in the railroad depot in Indianapolis. The train that brought them let out a long, gasping wheeze from its steam engine as its great iron wheels ground against the tracks and pulled out again, continuing its journey north.

"What are we supposed to do now?" asked George Kendley, sending his youthful gaze across the shadowy corners of the grimy depot. The sunlight faded outside, and George's question echoed, trailing off inside the darkening building. None of the adults in the group answered.

The Kendleys had been told they could find work in Indianapolis, but no company representatives waited to meet them at the station, and they didn't see broadsides tacked on the walls announcing available jobs. The blue-coated soldiers on guard in the depot offered no guidance or encouragement, and the few well-dressed passengers who descended from other cars stared at the ragged group and walked away, shaking their heads.

Mary Kendley wanted to cry. She was tired and couldn't remember the last time she slept a whole night without getting frightened by strange noises. Her skirts were heavy with dampness and dirt, and she couldn't remember the last time she was completely clean from head to toe. But she reached deep within herself and pulled up a smile, because Sara Jane had been holding the family together. Mary knew she had to remain cheerful. Tempers were short enough these days. "Now, George, that's a very good question," she said.

"Why don't you just answer it yourself, and then we'll all know what to do." George answered her with a smirk.

"Well, we certainly can't set out wandering the streets at this hour," said Sara Jane. "Maybe we should just spread our quilts here. We can venture out in the morning. Hugh and George, you go with the other boys and see if you can find a vendor outside with something hot, maybe some broth. We have two biscuits left we can share."

Sara Jane had no idea the evening they arrived in Indianapolis how many, many days during the next few months the four of them, and other refugees, would wander the city streets in search of work and food. She had no idea they would make their way back to the train depot each night because there was no place else to go. The sweeper and soldiers kicked the refugees out each morning. Fortunately, they did not have the heart to shoo the homeless people out after they returned each evening. It was far too cold to sleep on the streets or in the fields.

Hugh worked an hour one day helping an elderly man load a wagon. Next morning, George took the few coins he had earned and bought apples at the market. Selling them in the depot seemed like a wonderful idea until one of the soldiers saw him. "You rebels ain't allowed to sell stuff," he said. "Try that again, and out you go."

Samuel Farr found a job in Indianapolis and moved Rebecca Jane and Jonathan to a boarding house. Jonathan's fall off the army wagon left him with a broken jaw, his only serious injury. It was healing some, but it troubled him the rest of his life.

Almost every week, Samuel brought a basket of food to the thirty-five or forty millworkers still sleeping at the train depot. Whenever they asked Samuel about other jobs, he shook his head sadly and said, " 'Mebbe next month.' That's all they say when I ask."

And so the bone-chilling winter of 1864 passed. Some of the more skilled millworkers found jobs and left the train depot for better lodging. Several of the workers tried to take other shelter, but there was no heat in the empty sheds they found so they returned to the depot. Occasionally kindly women came to the depot bringing small parcels of food or cloth for the refugees. They apologized for not bringing clothes and blankets, but the times were hard for their families too. They told Sara Jane and Mary Kendley they were trying to get the government to do something, but so few supplies were available and most everything was going to the soldiers.

At Christmastime the women brought pairs of stockings for the little girls and a few scarves they had knitted themselves. They brought tiny scented bags for the women and even a roasted chicken wrapped in cloth. They apologized again and again that they could not do more.

Finally, just after dawn one morning in January 1865, the refugees heard a commotion outside the depot entrance. Two of the soldiers came and told everyone to line up at the entrance, where there was a wagon. At long last, the Union government was delivering ration tins and blankets. One of the women who had brought the refugees food and gifts at Christmas was standing outside, her hands buried in a muff and her breath puffing white clouds into the chilly air. "We're working on a place for you to stay," she announced. "Just hold on for another week or so. I'll let you know if we get it and . . . and when its ready."

The woman left, but for the first time in many months the refugees had enough food, clean blankets, and hope of a better place to stay. Mary Kendley wanted to believe they would find new shelter, but she had been hoping for so many things. She decided to wait and see—without the hope.

But the woman's promise was not false. A few days later she returned and announced with trembling excitement in her voice, "You can't all go at once, but pack up what you have, and we'll take a wagonload of you at a time. Tonight you'll sit in chairs at a table for your dinner, and you'll sleep on clean cots."

The southern millworker families welcomed the woman's words. The anonymous, frustrating role they had been playing in the long war was wearing them down. They were tired and ready to begin new lives—at least until there was some closure to the war that would allow them to go home.

It looked more and more as if that closure would favor the Union rather than the Confederacy. Sherman's advance into Georgia, the very event that forced these people north, helped turn that tide.

Newspapers reported that Abraham Lincoln had been re-elected president of the United States in November, largely because of renewed confidence in the war. That confidence was based on Sherman's capture of Atlanta in September and the start of his infamous march toward the sea. Rumors circulated that Savannah had fallen just before Christmas and that Sherman had turned northward toward the Carolinas.

There also was news of Confederate defeats at Franklin, Tennessee, and Nashville in December. Everyone on both sides of the war was tired, but President Lincoln was determined to prove his point about the Union, and the fighting continued.

No specific evidence exists that Roswell millworkers were among those who moved gratefully into the large building provided by the Charitable Association and its dedicated ladies in Indianapolis in January 1865. But family traditions, census records, and obituary notices suggest many of the displaced Roswell residents were in Indianapolis at exactly the time the building opened. This refugee center allowed at least fifty people to eat, sleep, and groom themselves in comfort for the first time in more than six months.

Job opportunities for the millworkers remained sporadic, but the prospects gradually improved. The North began to look beyond the war as the winter months of 1864 withered away and spring lightened the air. Early April 1865 brought word not only of Lee's surrender to Grant in Appomattox, but also of the assassination of Abraham Lincoln. These events were followed by the quick capitulation of rebel troops in Alabama. Northern businessmen reasoned it would not be long before they could return their companies to civilian manufacturing.

Various reports from the final approach of the war's end suggest millworkers from Roswell and Sweetwater Creek found work in Seymour and Shelbyville, Indiana, southeast of Indianapolis. It is difficult, however, to determine whether those reports are accurate. Although 1870 census records for those towns list a number of Georgia-born farmhands and domestic servants who came to Indiana after 1860, none of the names match those of people who worked in the Roswell and Sweetwater Creek mills in 1860. If any

Cannelton, Indiana, was a good mill location because of plentiful, cheap coal. This mill was strikingly different from the mills in Georgia—at least four times as large and powered by steam. It is doubtful that the Cannelton mill was in full operation when some of the Georgia workers and their families first crossed into Indiana in late 1864. *(Photo from the hill above the Cannelton mill by Barney Cook)*

of the millworkers did settle and work for a time in Seymour or Shelbyville, they would have had to arrive in Roswell after the 1860 census and/or leave Indiana before the 1870 census.

The same was true in New Albany where John T. Creed established a woolen mill in 1862. By 1870 this facility manufactured woolen and cotton goods, employing almost two hundred people, including fourteen-year-old Franklin Boyd. His fifty-year-old mother, Elizabeth, was from South Carolina, and all five of her children were Georgia-born. But there are no Boyds on the 1860 census listing for either Roswell or Sweetwater Creek. Elizabeth Boyd and her family probably came to Indiana from another location in Georgia.

The same is likely true of Georgia Hanson, a twenty-five-year-old woolen weaver who worked in a New Albany mill in 1870. Both she and her forty-eight-year-old mother, Elizabeth, were born in Georgia but not listed as residents of Roswell or Sweetwater Creek in 1860.

The Indiana Cotton Mills facility in Cannelton returned to full blast in early May 1865 after another shutdown. In anticipation of the reopening, an agent from the mill traveled to Indianapolis and perhaps to Louisville in search of "an increased supply of women," as one local newspaper phrased it. Mill supervisors liked to hire women and girls to work their spindles and looms because they took a more delicate approach with these tasks.

A number of Roswell millworkers found their way to Cannelton in early 1865, possibly through company agents. Although no existing written records detail exactly when they made the journey from Indianapolis or how they made it, we do know that Sara Jane and Mary Kendley and their two younger brothers, Thomas Hugh and George, arrived in Cannelton that spring. Lavina Fretwell and Lively Moore and their children probably did too, along with Elizabeth James and her daughter, Sarah. The family of Pleasant Bryan(t) stayed in Indianapolis until 1868.

The cotton mill at Cannelton was strikingly different from the Roswell and Sweetwater Creek mills in Georgia, even though it was built during the same era before the Civil War. The workmen who constructed the Cannelton mill in 1849 did not have to build cofferdams to dry out a section of riverbed so they could erect a dam for a waterwheel. The Cannelton mill did not rely on water power. Coal-fueled boilers produced the steam used to drive its spindles and looms. Cannelton also was blessed with a seemingly inexhaustible supply of cannel coal to fire those boilers. The Cannelton mill's primary need for the water in the river was transportation—first for the ginned cotton coming up from Mississippi and Louisiana and then for the textiles woven from that cotton.

The Indiana builders also didn't have to fire red bricks for the upper stories of the mill because, unlike the Georgia mills, Cannelton was constructed almost entirely of native gray-brown sandstone chiseled from the high cliff behind the town. The size of the Cannelton mill dwarfed almost anything in existence in Georgia in 1849. It rose five stories high and had square footage roughly four times that of the first Roswell mill building. Twin hundred-foot towers rose even higher on either side of the main entrance, making the Cannelton mill appear even more imposing.

In the 1850s and 1860s steamboat travelers on the Ohio River sometimes mistook the Cannelton mill for an important government building because of its stately architecture, dignified setting of trees, and lawns surrounded by a paling fence. Even though the trees, lawns, and fence disappeared long ago, the mill still stands solemnly beside the river.

The Cannelton mill was quite modern for its time, and its construction incorporated a number of fire-safety factors, including wide stairways with easy descent, along with one hundred fifty feet of fire hose in each of its workrooms. Two cisterns at the rear of the mill held more than one hundred thousand gallons of water that could be pumped quickly.

The north tower had a water closet on each floor. In addition to its "privy" function, this tower provided perfect ventilation. The privy lids were opened morning and evening to create a powerful draft designed to suck flammable lint out of the attic and workrooms and down through a tunnel to the chimney. Connected to the main building by a tunnel, the mill's chimney once stood so tall that it dwarfed the imposing towers at the mill's front entrance.

Lumbermen harvested sixty-foot beams in upper Ohio Valley forests and floated them downriver to be installed between the floors in the Cannelton mill. Woodworkers reportedly used Philippine mahogany to fashion the deep red-toned pillars that still support those massive beams. One businessman has offered Historic Cannelton Inc. five thousand dollars apiece for those pillars if the mill is ever torn down, but the heritage organization is determined to preserve the historic structure.

During the mill's prime, steam drove the machinery and heated the workrooms. At great expense sometime after 1854, the owners installed gaslights high on the inside walls so the millworkers could continue their twelve-hour shifts in shorter winter months.

The Cannelton mill did not meet the financial expectations of its original owners, partly because construction costs totaled more than three times the amount they estimated. The high cost of labor in what was then the "West," along with Cannelton's somewhat remote location, probably contributed to the inflated construction costs. The owners sold the mill, and buyers reorganized it in 1853. For many years the Cannelton mill was the largest industrial building in Indiana and west of the Allegheny Mountains.

One day in spring 1865, Mary Kendley stared at the massive front of the Cannelton mill. She leaned her head back and shaded her eyes to see the top of it. The sunshine beamed down from an unusually cloudless sky that day, and the building cast a slanted shadow extending beyond the cluster of Roswell workers gathered

Much of Cannelton, Indiana, was built from the plentiful sandstone found in the area, including St. Michael's Catholic Church and the narrow, steep-roofed houses that still stand on many streets. *(Photo by Barney Cook)*

in front of it. Mary wasn't quite sure what she expected, but it certainly was not this giant. It minimized the effect of everything else in this small town where all the streets slanted southward toward the Ohio River.

Sandstone, that's what someone had told her it was made of. She had never seen so much sand-colored stone before. The whole town appeared carved from one huge slab of the stuff—the Catholic church up the hill, the skinny houses with their steep roofs, and this scary mill where she was supposed to begin work the next morning. The mill in Roswell was hot and cramped at times, but there was no way to get lost in it. And its redbrick walls certainly were more cheerful than the ones at the Cannelton mill.

The Yankee agent who brought them to the mill talked fast just like he walked, and Mary had to concentrate hard to understand what he said. "Now that big bell up there will sound out to let you know when it's time to come to work each morning. You get forty-five minutes for breakfast and the same for lunch. Bring your own food. You'll be paid by the cut or the bolt each week, and your lodging rent—I'll show you the lodgings when we finish here—will be deducted before you get your due. And we don't tolerate any crying about wages. Ours are the best around here, so just be glad you have 'em. Any kids who are twelve years old can work too. Just give us names, and we'll let you know when we need 'em. Any questions? If so, save 'em till next week when you've worked six shifts and you know what to ask."

No one said a word when the wiry little agent finished his speech. Sara Jane caught Mary's eye and shook her head. Mary smiled and turned her gaze away from the mill toward the wide, peaceful river. It was only a few hundred yards away, with Kentucky on the other side. Kentucky was the South, but with everything so muddled it didn't seem that way. Mary wondered if she would ever get back to Georgia, where people's voices and manners were familiar, where the food tasted right, and where she knew what was what. Would she ever see Matilda and John and their families again?

Sara Jane tapped her shoulder. "You all right?" she asked. Mary nodded. She knew it was time to buckle down and create a new life in this place, if only for a little while. She and Sara Jane owed themselves that, and George and Thomas Hugh too. They had no money, and the government had no system in place for returning the refugees to Georgia. Perhaps in a year or so they could return.

On an early evening in June 1865, Mary Kendley strolled up one of the streets in Cannelton—up away from the river, perhaps toward the Methodist church or the grocery. She had not thought about Roswell in several weeks. Suddenly the gray eyes of a tall, gaunt man brought back all the fear and anger she felt before she was forced to leave Georgia. Those eyes and the man's blue

Washington Street in Cannelton, Indiana, looks today much as it did when Mary Kendley encountered one of Sherman's raiders on a Cannelton street in the summer of 1865. *(Photo by Barney Cook)*

uniform also brought back the vow she had made to herself—
to remember every last one of General Sherman's raiders who
invaded Roswell and herded her and her family to the sweltering
town square.

Mary stopped abruptly on the dusty footpath, almost pitching
forward. She had to reach out and steady herself against the thin
porch post of a building. Peering out from beneath her bonnet, she
looked up into the startled eyes of the soldier.

" 'Scuse me, ma'am," he said, moving slightly aside and
politely removing his wide-brimmed leather hat.

Mary stepped directly in front of him, planting her feet squarely
and placing her hands on her hips. "You don't remember me, do
you?" she said. "You don't remember any of us."

"No, ma'am, can't say that I do," he answered, glancing quickly
beyond Mary's shoulder.

Mary cleared her throat. "Roswell, Georgia, last July," she said,
drawing out her answer with the thickest southern accent she could
manage.

"Ohhhh," said the man. "Well now, that's all over. That was
quite a while back."

"It most certainly is *not* over," said Mary. "The war may be over,
but you're still wearing that uniform and we're still suffering all
the consequences." She could hear her voice rising louder beyond
her control, but she couldn't stop herself. She could feel her temper
rising to a solid lump at the top of her throat. "You're up here in
Indiana because you want to be, but me and my family got forced
up here, and now we're stuck here. We weren't Confederate soldiers. You had no right to take us out of Georgia."

The man glanced nervously beyond Mary's shoulder again. "I'm
real sorry about all that, ma'am, but we were just following orders.
It was wartime, and that's how those things go; but you can go on
back home now, can't you?"

The lump in Mary's throat was so tight she almost couldn't stand
it. "Well, perhaps, but to what? I've heard what all you raiders did
to the rest of Georgia after you loaded us in those wagons and sent

Although she remained in Cannelton, Indiana, after the war, Mary Kendley married a southerner—Albert Alexander May, who fought for the Confederacy as a member of the 4th Florida Infantry of Franklin County. Albert May came to Cannelton sometime after his release in February 1865 from a Union prison camp at the Indiana state fairgrounds. *(Family portrait of Mary Kendley May and Albert Alexander May used with permission of Margaret May Schank)*

us off to Marietta. There's nothin' left to go home to. Maybe you were following orders, but you followed them too well I think."

As Mary fumbled for words to finish what she wanted to say, she felt a soft touch on her arm. She turned and looked into the dark, deep-set eyes of a young man about her height, someone she had never seen before. He started to speak, but she was still on fire with anger. Jerking her arm away, she turned back to the Yankee soldier. "You enjoyed burning our mill and turning us all out of our homes. I could see it in your eyes. You're nothing but a bunch of . . . a bunch of . . ." Her voice trailed off because she couldn't find words terrible enough to match what she felt.

"I think you'd better move on now, officer," said the young man in a distinctly Georgian accent that warmed her ears. He grasped Mary's elbow firmly before adding, "You've upset this young lady quite enough."

"But she . . ."

"I said I think it best you walk on by now, sergeant," said the young man.

The soldier looked at the young man, then at Mary, and nodded. He replaced the leather hat on his head, turned, thrust his hands into his pockets, and walked on down toward the river. As he did so, Albert May tipped his hat, smiled, and introduced himself to Mary Kendley.

The key to freedom for both civilian and military prisoners of the Union during the Civil War was often the signing of an oath of allegiance to the United States. Captured civilians, like the Georgia millworkers, were usually released and allowed to find work if they signed an oath. Especially for families, it was difficult not to choose an option that might provide a healthier environment—although some discovered worse conditions when they tried to survive on their own. Military prisoners who signed an oath also were released. Earlier in the war, some chose to ignore such an oath and return to the South to fight again. If they were recaptured, however, death was an immediate penalty. Later in the war, as defeat loomed, some signed the oath and remained in the North to avoid further conscription by the Confederacy.

Oaths of allegiance, like the one signed by Albert May, became more standardized after President Abraham

United States of America.

I, _Albert A May Corp Co. B. 4th Fla Infy_ of the County of _Franklin_. State of _Florida_, do solemnly swear, in presence of Almighty God, that I will henceforth faithfully support, protect, and defend the Constitution of the United States, and the Union of the States thereunder; and that I will, in like manner, abide by and faithfully support all acts of Congress passed during the existing rebellion with reference to slaves, so long and so far as not repealed, modified, or held void by Congress, or by decision of the Supreme Court; and that I will, in like manner, abide by and faithfully support all proclamations of the President made during the existing rebellion having reference to slaves, so long and so far as not modified or declared void by decision of the Supreme Court: So help me God.

Albert A. May

Subscribed and sworn to before me, at _Camp Morton Ind._, this _17th_ day of _February_, A. D. 186_5_.

The above-named has _Dark_ complexion, _Brown_ hair, and _Hazel_ eyes; and is _5_ feet _5 1/2_ inches high.

(Photocopy of original used with the permission of Mary Ida Robson Powers of Tell City, Indiana)

103

ROLL OF PRISONERS OF WAR					T/
WHEN RECEIVED.	NO.	NAMES—IN ALPHABETICAL ORDER (BY REGIMENTS AND COMPANIES.)	RANK OR TOWN.	REGIMENT OR COUNTY AND STATE.	
Aug 7th 1863	1976	Lacey J. W.	✓	Private	2nd Arkansas	3
	1974 5	Lindley J. M.	✓		9th Texas	9
	6	Lewis A B	✓		3d Miss	6
	9 1980	Langdon John	✓			
	8	Looper William	✓			
	9	Laperenda Alphonse	✓	Corporal	25th La	A
	1980 2	Lamper H.	✓		13th "	
	3 1	Lee J. M	✓		9th Texas	
	4 2	Mace G A	✓	Sergeant	60th N. C	
	5 3	McGee S. H	✓	"	41st Tenn	
	4	Moore P. S	✓	"	3d La	
	7 5	McDonald James	✓	"	2nd Ky	E
	6	Mosely A. T.	✓	Corporal	12th La	2
	7 1990 8	McQuilton Robert	✓	"	25th Ga	J
	8	May A. A.	✓	"	7th Florida	B
	9	Moulin C	✓	Drummer	13th La	C
	2 1990	Morris John W.	✓	"	"	A

This "Roll of Prisoners of War" is from Camp Morton, Indiana, a Union prisoner of war camp located on the state fairgrounds in Indianapolis during the Civil War. Albert Alexander May is the fifteenth prisoner listed as having been received on August 7, 1863. He had served as a corporal in Company B of

Lincoln signed his amnesty proclamation on December 8, 1863. Lincoln was eager to find a way to invite southerners back into loyal citizenship. Those who signed were pardoned, and their property was not confiscated. For most southerners, swearing loyalty to the United States was an extremely bitter pill. Some justified signing as appropriate once it was clear that the Confederacy would be defeated militarily. Some signed so they could stay in the North, where the 1st Florida regiment and had been captured near Jackson, Mississippi, in July 1863. *(Photocopy of original used courtesy of the National Archives and Records Administration.)*

jobs and supplies were more plentiful. Others vowed never to sign. In civilian refugee prison houses like those in Louisville and in military prisons like Camp Chase and Camp Morton, debates on the issue were long and agonizing. During the war and even long after it was over, many Confederate loyalists continued to regard anyone who had signed a loyalty oath to the United States as a traitor to the noble cause of the South.

This page from the "Descriptive Book of the Confederate Prisoners of War
Released from U.S. Military Prison, Camp Morton, Indiana" lists Albert May
as Prisoner #800. It gives his age as twenty-two and states that he was a
farmer from Franklin, Florida, when he enlisted in Apalachicola. He was 5 feet,
5½ inches tall and had a dark complexion, hazel eyes, and brown hair. The
record indicates the date of the order for his release as February 15, 1865. His
actual release on February 17 was contingent upon his signing an oath of
allegiance to the United States. Had Albert May known how quickly circumstances at Camp Morton were about to change, it is likely he would not have
signed the oath. Just a few days after he signed, five hundred disabled prisoners
were released in Indiana without having to sign. Later that spring regular
prisoner exchanges like those at Camp Chase began to occur. By the summer
of 1865 Camp Morton was completely empty. *(Photocopy of original used
courtesy of the National Archives and Records Administration)*

CHAPTER 10

STRAWBERRY MANNA

When Walter Washington Stewart hugged his daughter Synthia Catherine and the rest of his family goodbye in Louisville in August 1864, he promised to come back to get them. "I don't really know what they're going to do with me," he told his wife, Lizzie, "but if I live, I'll get word to you somehow. I'll let you know where I am and try to write to you. If they . . . when they let me loose, I'll get back here just as soon as I can."

Walter did not know when he might be released. He had no more illusions that the South would win the war, and he had no idea how long it would drag on before a Confederate defeat became a reality.

Shortly after Walter's all-too-brief reunion with his family, he and James Mozley, along with James Mauldin and John Smith, crossed the Ohio River to Jeffersonville, Indiana, under armed guard. From there they traveled by train to Cincinnati and then to Columbus, Ohio.

During the two days Walter and his fellow captives were imprisoned in Louisville, the sympathetic ladies of that Union-occupied southern city gave them baskets of food and cheering words. The ladies didn't mind that the Confederate soldiers were ragged and dirty because they admired the rebels' chivalry and bravery. But the rebel prisoners' experience was totally different when they stepped from the train car in Cincinnati during a break in their journey. Cincinnati was unlike Louisville, which was basically southern but Union-occupied. Cincinnati was very obviously Union territory through and through. Men, women, and children crowded the train depot to jeer at the prisoners and point at their sorry condition. "Serves you right for defying the Constitution," a woman in a black bonnet shouted out like a shrill crow as Walter waited with his comrades at the water barrel.

After enduring another dismal train ride from Cincinnati into the heartland of Ohio, Walter and his fellow prisoners followed their guards on a quick march from the train depot through the streets of Columbus to Camp Chase. Again the Confederates suffered the jeers of unsympathetic Yankee crowds: "Where's your Jeff Davis now, you wretched rebels? No slaves here to wipe your ugly noses!"

No written record exists of Walter Stewart's personal experiences during the long months he spent in Camp Chase, but they were probably similar to those of surgeon John H. King, who was captured in 1864. In 1904 King wrote *Three Hundred Days in a Yankee Prison,* a memoir describing his incarceration at Camp Chase.

Walter Stewart arrived at this bleak prisoner-of-war camp at a much warmer time of the year than King did. Although Walter suffered the same primitive conditions as King, he was less concerned about needing a heavy blanket or an overcoat, and the ground under his bare feet was not as cruel. Walter probably heard the same exclamation King did though: "Fresh fish!" That was the term long-time prisoners at Camp Chase used to describe newcomers.

Even before they reached the entrance to the camp, Walter and the other fresh fish felt the ever-watchful eyes of the sentinels who carried bayoneted guns and paced the walkway at the top of the high, wooden stockade surrounding Camp Chase. Early afternoon the day he arrived, Walter was taken to his quarters in a long, narrow shanty with bare bunks down each side and a "kitchen" at one end. At mealtime Walter and the other prisoners picked up tin plates of food slid through a narrow slit in the wall between the kitchen area and bunk room. Hungry as he was, Walter could barely choke down the horrid-smelling slop pushed through to him each day.

James Mozley bunked in the same quarters as Walter, but Mauldin and Smith were marched to other barracks. "Do we get a change of clothes? Or a blanket?" asked Mozley, staring at the bare wooden bunk where he was supposed to sleep.

The guard looked him up and down and made a rumbling noise in his throat. "No new clothes until the ones you're wearin' rot off of you," he announced, "and no new blankets till the frost sets in. Doesn't your rebel army tell you to bring your own supplies when you come to prison?" The guard was proud of his sarcasm and laughed hard until he began to cough.

The guards gave Walter and the others tin cups for water. "When you go to the pump, you fill your cup and drink," the guards told them. "And you drink every drop. We ain't got water here to spare for rinsing. You throw any water on the ground by that pump, and you just might get yourself shot like the last miserable rebel who tried to rinse his cup before drinking."

Veteran prisoners warned the fresh fish to "take the guards seriously when they hollered 'Lights out!'" If the lamps in the barracks didn't go out immediately, the guards sometimes fired into the bunk room. And if they saw a light during the night—no matter that someone might be sick and need attention—they'd fire shots.

The veteran prisoners also warned Walter and the others about possible spies among them. There were onetime Confederates who passed along information about escape attempts in exchange for better food and easier treatment. " 'Razorbacks,' we call 'em," explained a veteran. "You can try escaping if you want to, but those who fail reap all kinds of rewards." When Mozley asked what those rewards were, the prisoner painted a dismal picture of would-be escapees hanging by their thumbs or doing hard labor with a ball and chain around their ankles. Some escapees were even bucked, gagged, and left on the ground for hours at a time for a prescribed number of days.

In spite of these threatened horrors, Walter considered escape. The memory of his recent visit with Lizzie and his children in Louisville was fresh in his mind. He worried that one of them would get sick before he could remove them from the refugee prison and get them eating right and sleeping again like they should.

But the stockade rose at least twenty feet above ground level, and the Yankees made sure it was well lit at night. The sentinels could see every inch of the camp, and twelve-man detachments continuously guarded the strong double-gate entrance. Walter heard some of the prisoners whispering at night that they might be better off to charge that gate. "We're all gonna die in here anyway," they said, "just more slowly and with all these scurrying vermin for mourners."

Walter didn't agree. He had everything to live for, no matter how miserable it was day to day. And maybe he still had his land back in Sweetwater Creek. If he, Lizzie, and the children could just get back, he would find some chickens and plant a small crop.

Through the long fall of 1864 and the bone-chilling dampness of the winter months, Walter set himself small goals each morning. He tried to stay healthy and not lose hope. He and James Mozley daydreamed about how it would be if they ever got home to Georgia. They tried not to notice the blank stares of their fellow prisoners who withdrew past caring. Men didn't live long once they began staring like that.

In February 1865 a rumor rumbled through Camp Chase that arrangements for a prisoner exchange were underway. Even men with the blank stares roused themselves enough to speculate about who might soon be marched out of the wretched prison. The guards laughed at the prisoners' eager questions, insisting the rumors were false. But one bitterly cold morning near the end of the month, the guards grouped the prisoners into divisions. Over a period of three days, the guards marched several divisions of prisoners out through the prison camp's double gates.

Walter did not see James Mauldin and John Smith when they marched out, but he heard they boarded trains for Wheeling, Virginia, and then Baltimore. Walter also heard that the Confederates would be traded for Union prisoners at a wharf on the James River. "I'm glad they got out," Walter told James Mozley, "but knowing they did makes staying in here all the harder."

Walter also heard rumors that the war might end soon and that they would be released. "Don't be too sure," one fellow prisoner warned. "These Yanks might not want us telling the whole world how they treated us."

"All's fair, unfortunately," said another prisoner. "I hear the guards in our prisoner-of-war camps haven't treated Yankee prisoners any better."

Fall and winter 1864 passed just as slowly for Walter's family at the female prison in Louisville as they had for him at Camp Chase in Ohio. Although the female prison provided better conditions for Lizzie and the children than Walter's prisoner-of-war camp, the southern women and children still suffered and the Louisville Refugee Commission worked to make daily life better for them.

In September 1864 the commission once again begged the residents of Louisville for contributions. A newspaper editorial suggested that nine-tenths of the female prisoners still living in the refugee house on Broadway suffered from a typhoid-like disease. The newspaper article reported that their bedding, which was rotten with filth and vermin, had to be replaced and that the prisoners had to be moved to cleaner quarters. The Refugee Commission asked the ladies of Louisville to think of their love for their own children and bring whatever bedding and clothing they could spare to one of several stores on Market Street.

During that same week in September, Dr. Mary E. Walker arrived in Louisville "for duty with female prisoners in this city." The U.S. Assistant Surgeon General, acting on Sherman's instructions, assigned Walker to the refugee prison—perhaps in an effort to improve the health conditions. Ther is no documentation to prove that Walker interacted with specific families mentioned in this book; however, her administration coincides with the dates of their confinement. Records from this period that are available reflect both fact and rumor about the conditions these refugees experienced.

Walker, a surgeon with a medical degree from Syracuse Medical College in New York, was divorced from a fellow doctor. The independent Walker determined her gender would not keep her from a successful career, but her determination created a stir wherever she went. Like Amelia Bloomer, Walker favored dress reform for women and wore full trousers gathered scandalously at the ankle under a short, skirted jacket. She parted her dark hair in the middle, pulled back over her ears. Walker's severe hairstyle, combined with her dark eyebrows and rather prominent nose, gave her a definite no-nonsense appearance.

At the beginning of the Civil War in 1861, twenty-nine-year-old Walker left her private medical practice and tried to enlist in the Union Army as a surgeon. When she was refused a commission, she served as a nurse to frontline soldiers wounded at Fredericksburg and Chickamauga. But she continued to badger Washington politicians for an official physician's appointment. During this period she also organized a relief society for needy visitors to Washington and other northern cities. These visitors were often southern women who arrived to comfort their wounded and captured Confederate husbands with little money to pay for lodging and food.

Walker finally received her appointment as a regimental assistant surgeon with Union Army pay, but without an officer's commission. She reported to the front at Chattanooga early in 1864, where the Confederates soon captured her as a spy. The Confederates were shocked to find a female doctor among their Union prisoners, and one captain wrote to his wife of his amusement that the Yankee nation could produce such a "thing," dressed in full uniform, not good-looking, and with a very sharp tongue.

The Confederates sent Walker to Richmond, where southern women gawked in disbelief as she was led through the streets to imprisonment at a place called Castle Thunder. The *Richmond Examiner* referred to her as "the Yankee Surgeoness" and stated that she seemed "anxious to make any concessions which are demanded of her, save that of her title to doctorship and the right to attire herself in men's apparel."

When Walker assumed her duties with the female prisoners in Louisville, she was still a doctor and wore her bloomer-style uniform. A number of written accounts suggest she was not well liked by the women prisoners. There are several tales of her outright cruelty, including one that Walker did not allow the imprisoned women and children to eat a Christmas dinner prepared for them by charitable ladies of Louisville.

Controversy between Walker and her female prisoner patients raged on into 1865, finally escalating into an outright disturbance that prompted the doctor to write a letter of explanation to the Commandant of Post in Louisville on January 15. Walker's methodical, defensive explanation of prison rules and actions presents a strikingly different point of view from the account of a female prisoner who was arrested in her home in north Georgia and sent to the Louisville prison.

The woman from north Georgia complained that Walker replaced the male cooks at the prison with totally incompetent women who had such poor hygiene that the prisoners could not stand to eat the food they prepared. Walker, however, told the commandant she simply insisted there be no familiarity between male cooks and female prisoners, and that someone else actually ordered the male cooks to be replaced with women.

Addressing the issue of her abusing the children prisoners, Walker's letter to the commandant explained that the women prisoners neglected their children and that she would not stand for it. She described one woman who put her baby in the crib at night and then ignored it until morning no matter how much it cried. "I finally took the crib out of the room and compelled [the woman] to take [the baby] into the bed with her and take care of it."

Walker wrote about another woman who had two children under the age of four and did not keep them clean. Walker reported that the woman said she wished her children were dead. "I told her if she did not pay them sanitary attention, I would have them given to someone who would," wrote Walker.

Walker also told of a woman prisoner who tried to hang her niece with a rope to scare her into obedience. Walker wrote that she told the prisoner she wouldn't stand for this behavior, and explained in her letter that the niece was one of three orphans whose father had died in the rebel army and whose mother had died in the refugee prison in October 1864.

The Georgia woman said she was told that Walker had children of her own, but she couldn't believe that was true because "no mother could have done what I saw her do to a little two-year-old baby—the child of one of the prisoners." The woman described the baby sitting at the head of the stairs holding a piece of bread when the doctor came along and screamed for the baby to get out of her way. The woman went on to report that when the baby didn't move, Walker kicked the baby down the stairs.

Walker's letter to the Louisville Commandant of Post mentions several other rules she enforced at the prison. She demanded cleanliness. She did not allow the women to sing rebel songs or engage in disloyal conversation. And she read any letters they received from rebel visitors. Walker also wrote that she handcuffed one woman for two hours for calling the guard a bad name, threatening to kill two other prisoners, and daring the doctor to come upstairs in the building.

Walker also mentioned that she locked several women in an outside storehouse for waving their handkerchiefs and yelling Jeff Davis's name at rebel prisoners passing by outside. According to the Georgia woman, the rebel prisoners passed by on Christmas morning, and she and others waved their handkerchiefs at them. Walker had observed this and promptly put all of them in a dungeon for the rest of Christmas Day, the prisoner claimed.

It is not easy to determine whether either account gives an accurate picture of Dr. Mary Walker and how she treated the female prisoners in Louisville. "If ever a fiend in human guise walked this earth it did it in that woman's body," wrote the woman from Georgia. "Her character was a combination of brutality, malice, and cowardice." In her letter to the commandant, Walker countered the woman's account by saying, "Give them their filth, unrestrained disloyalty, and immorality and it will be satisfactory times with them. I am an eye sore to them, and they want men cooks again, and a man doctor . . . Colonel Fairleigh has learned my true motives for all that I have done, and appreciates the trying position I hold, and all my greatest superior officers have confidence in my having done *well* under all circumstances, and that confidence is *merited.*"

In spring 1865 Walker asked to be relieved of her duty at the Female Military Prison in Louisville so she could return to a medical position at the front. Her request was granted on March 22, 1865, and Walker proceeded without delay to Nashville. She retired from the Union Army in June with a pension and was awarded the Medal of Honor by President Andrew Johnson. After the war, Walker worked for a while at a newspaper office in New York and then returned to medical practice in Washington, proudly wearing her medal and ignoring the harassment and criticism she incurred for wearing trousers.

Synthia Catherine Stewart and her family may or may not have been at the Female Military Prison when Walker issued her stern orders and angered the refugees. Many years later, Synthia Catherine told her grandson that she and the rest of her family left the Louisville prison after her father was sent to Camp Chase. Synthia Catherine's mother, Lizzie, found bookkeeping work with the government and used her earnings to rent housing for her and the children in Louisville. Lizzie also arranged for the children to go to a nearby school.

If Lizzie had signed an oath of allegiance to the U.S. government, she could have moved the children out of the prison and begun work in the fall of 1864. If Lizzie had not signed an oath, she and the children probably would have remained in the refugee prison until April 1865, when the military commander ordered an unconditional release of all remaining prisoners.

Robert E. Lee surrendered to Ulysses S. Grant at Appomattox Court House in southwestern Virginia on April 9, 1865. On May 16, Walter Stewart and James Mozley were released from Camp Chase.

One morning toward the end of May 1865, when Synthia Catherine and her older sister Sarah arrived at their school in Louisville, their teacher called them aside. "I think your father is coming here to Louisville today," she whispered.

Synthia Catherine tilted her head and narrowed her eyes at this northern lady. "How do you know that?" she asked. Sarah poked her hard in the ribs and made a loud, shushing noise. "Well how can she know?" asked Synthia Catherine, turning toward her sister. "She doesn't even know what he looks like."

The teacher smiled—she was used to little girls. "Well," she said, "I went across the river to [New] Albany, [Indiana,] last evening to see a friend, and I stayed over there all night. Early this morning when I was waiting at the wharf for the boat to arrive to take me back across the river, I saw some soldiers standing there. They weren't Yankee soldiers either."

The teacher paused at this point, pretending that was all she planned to say.

"And?" asked Synthia Catherine.

Sarah jabbed her in the ribs again. "Please ignore my sister's rudeness," said Sarah primly. "We really do want to hear about the soldiers you saw, ma'am."

"Well," said the teacher, "I decided to be brave and talk to them, and there was one in particular that interested me. He was very tall and handsome, and I noticed something familiar about him. When I asked him his name, he told me it was Stewart."

Synthia Catherine let out a squeal and clapped her hand over her mouth as the teacher continued. "I told this rebel soldier that I have two little girls going to my school and that their name is also Stewart. And I told him that these two little girls look just like him, so I know that they . . . that you . . . are his children."

The teacher stopped talking, but Synthia Catherine could see her eyes sparkling. "And?" asked Synthia Catherine again; again Sarah jabbed her hard in the ribs.

"Well," said the teacher. "He won't be here directly. The soldiers had to wait for some papers they had to sign, but he is coming across the river this very day, and I'm sure your mother will send for you the moment he arrives. Now until then you get busy and do all your lessons just like the others."

"Yes, ma'am," Sarah answered. She grabbed Synthia Catherine's elbow and began to push her toward her desk.

"I think we better go back to our room at the boarding house right now," said Synthia Catherine. "Papa could be here already, and we don't even know."

"No," said Sarah. "We'll go home when Mama sends for us."

Synthia Catherine managed to get through the school day, but it wasn't easy. She didn't hear a word the teacher said because her mind was filled with memories of the long train trip that brought them to Louisville and the terrible months they spent in the refugee prison. Several times she closed her eyes and tried to picture the hollow tree where they hid her father's suit of clothes and the hollow stump where they packed the dishes around the water pitcher full of silver.

Papa was finally coming back, and now they would be able to go home again. They could dig up the china and the silver and have a chicken dinner without any Yankee soldiers stealing it.

Late in the afternoon the teacher was called from the classroom, and Synthia Catherine watched the doorway eagerly for her return. When the teacher came back into the room, she motioned Sarah and Synthia Catherine to her. "Now I can't just let you go home straight away—the rules won't let me. You'll have to write me a lesson first," she told them. "Each of you write three words on your slate and hand it to me, and then you can go on home and see your father."

Years later Synthia Catherine told her grandson that Sarah wrote three words very quickly and handed the slate back to the teacher. "I don't know what she wrote, and I never did," she said. "And I could have written just 'at' or 'et' or something simple, but for some reason, I wrote 'generalissimo' and 'hemorrhoid' and 'heterogeneous.' And then I handed the slate back to the teacher, and she just gave me sort of a sweet smile and didn't say anything at all to me."

Synthia Catherine and Sarah left the schoolhouse and started down the street to their boarding house. Synthia Catherine wanted to run all the way, but Sarah got a coughing fit and had to stop. "Don't you go on without me," she pleaded.

Synthia Catherine waited, but tapped her foot impatiently while Sarah cleared her throat. "I'm fine now," she said at last, and then they raced each other the last two blocks down the street.

They found their parents arm in arm in the middle of the one tiny room. They were laughing and crying at the same time, and they immediately drew Sarah and Synthia Catherine into a family circle of hugs that seemed to go on forever. Little Jim and Linnie Isabella were there too.

Several months passed before the Stewarts could think seriously about going home to Georgia. They couldn't afford a team and wagon even if they found one. And at first they couldn't find information about where the trains were running.

Walter moved into the boarding house with his family and searched for a job. He and Lizzie saved every penny they could and dreamed about going home. The older girls finished out the school year with the teacher who had spotted their father on the wharf.

Finally, in late summer or early fall 1865, Walter and Lizzie had saved enough money to take their family home to Georgia. They boarded a train and rumbled south over the same tracks that brought Lizzie, the children, and Uncle James north more than a year earlier. (Stewart family notes and the recording Synthia Catherine made many years later do not mention Uncle James returning with them to Georgia in 1865.)

A mostly colorless panorama raced past the train windows as the Stewarts made their way back through Kentucky and Tennessee. The war ripped apart the countryside, and everywhere the train stopped, Walter, Lizzie, and the children saw people with gray, unsmiling faces plodding along the tracks. The only bright colors they saw were on visiting Yankees. The northern men sported dapper suits, and the women, with hair piled high on their heads, wore flouncy satin dresses.

Walter Washington Stewart married Charlotte Elizabeth (Lizzie) Russell in 1851 when she was fifteen and he was twenty-three. They moved to the Sweet-water Creek area where he became "bossman" at the mill before enlisting in the Campbell Salt Springs Guards (Army of Tennessee) on March 4, 1862. *(Portrait of Walter Washington Stewart and Elizabeth Russell Stewart provided from a family history collection on file at Sweetwater Creek State Park)*

In north Georgia, Synthia Catherine told her father Uncle James's stories about the *General,* the locomotive Yankees stole and ran up the Western & Atlantic track toward Chattanooga. She also told him about how Sherman stopped the Confederate guerrillas from putting torpedoes on the tracks by forcing old rebels to ride along the rails in a boxcar.

"Did you ever see Sherman?" she asked her father when they reached Marietta. "Were you ever in a battle right where he was?"

"No, Honey, I never saw him with my own eyes, but Mama says you did."

Synthia Catherine nodded and told him how she got her Bible back from the Yankee soldier. When she pulled her Bible out of the little homespun sack she carried, Walter took the battered black book and placed it in his lap. He let it fall open by itself and then studied the pages for a moment, running his finger down the left side. He smiled as he read the words from Deuteronomy 8 to himself and then translated them into simpler language for his children. "God led those Israelites around in the wilderness for forty years. He did it to humble them and test them and make sure they would keep his commandments."

Walter stopped a moment, cleared his throat, and looked at each member of his family. "God humbled those Israelites and let them be hungry, but then he fed them with manna, a sort of bread that came down from heaven that none of them had ever seen before. He did that to remind them that he was their God and that he would take care of them if they lived by His Word."

Lizzie smiled and nodded. "Amen," she said, "and God kept us safe too and brought us home together."

Walking back to Sweetwater Creek from the railroad tracks, the Stewarts saw no one they knew before the war except old Mrs. Tutchstone, who wasn't sent north for some reason. She just shook her head and wouldn't talk at all when they asked her to tell them what all had happened during the year they were gone.

"Oh, Walter, no," Lizzie cried out when they finally reached their farm near Sweetwater Creek. The fences were down, and the trees that once shaded the yard were burned to stumps. The little house was standing, but there wasn't a full stick of furniture inside it. The doors were ripped from the front of the house and from the cabinets. "All used for Yankee campfires, most likely," said Walter.

Synthia Catherine stood in the wide-open doorway, staring out across the field that in earlier years would still have been green with vegetables her father planted. "Everything is dead. Absolutely everything!" she cried out. She couldn't see a green stem anywhere around her—just red clay dust and graying stubble where soft living things used to be. Not one bush was left standing in the yard, not even one little flower. She had hated the high stockade fence in Louisville and would have loved to knock it down, but it made her sad to see the posts of this fence lying around at crazy angles.

Walter came to the doorway of the house and rested his long arm across his daughter's shoulders. "Now don't you fret, Synthia Catherine," he said. "The Lord will provide, and don't you forget that. We'll get something growing here next summer. It will take a little time, that's all. And we'll get the house back together too."

Synthia Catherine shrugged. She wanted to believe him, but it was hard. It looked to her as if the whole world was dead.

That first night the Stewarts tacked a blanket across their front doorway and camped out, totally exhausted, in what was left of their home. The next morning Walter was up early, taking stock and figuring out what he could tear apart and put back together again to make a temporary front door. Little Jim shadowed his father's every step, with pride in his rebel father shining in his eyes.

Synthia Catherine rounded up Sarah and Linnie Isabella. "We're going after the silver and the crockery," she announced, hoisting an old quilt over her shoulder.

"Oh, Honey, do you think you can find that old tree?" asked Lizzie.

"Sure we can," said Synthia Catherine. "It's not far into the woods, on the slope above the creek, and there's a big gray rock right next to it."

"Everything's probably been carried off by now," said Lizzie. "A lot of time has passed. A lot of Yankees have marched through here and a lot of desperate Confederates too."

"It won't hurt to look," said Synthia Catherine.

"Now, Lizzie, don't let those girls go off into that woods by themselves," said Walter. "No telling who's around these days. All kinds of deserters from both armies." He put down the weathered board he'd been carrying and smiled. "Matter of fact, let's all go find that tree."

All of the Stewarts headed into the woods together. Synthia Catherine proudly led the way, dashing ahead on the path. She found the hollow tree just where she remembered it, next to the gray rock. Reaching it, she dropped to her knees and poked her head up into the hollow trunk. The rich smell inside reminded her of velvet black soil when one pulls up a plant beside a path in the woods. "It's still here!" she cried out, pulling her head back out and reaching for a stick to poke with. "The pouch is still here."

She and Sarah and Little Jim took turns poking up into the trunk until they finally dislodged the old leather saddlebag they had hidden there more than a year before.

"Well, I'll be Jeff Davis's housecat," Walter said as he unrolled the carefully tailored pants and jacket Lizzie made for him before the war. "Dry as a bone and not even a hole."

Lizzie smiled. "A little out of time for today, I'd say, but I can fix that."

Synthia Catherine watched her mother, who was already measuring with her eyes the snips she would take to make Walter's suit passable again. "Well if the clothes are still here and all okay, then . . ." Synthia Catherine started to say, but before she could finish her sentence, Sarah and Little Jim jumped up and ran on down the path. By the time she and Linnie Isabella and Walter and Lizzie caught up with them, they were already scraping away the leaves and brush around the hollow stump. As if by miracle, there lay all the Stewart crockery, covered with bits of leaves and soil but none of it in pieces. Sarah scraped more leaves from the top of the stump and dug into it with both hands. To her delight she felt the old water pitcher and wiggled it up into the dappled sunlight.

"My silver!" exclaimed Lizzie. "I never dared hope. Why, praise the Lord. When we get us a chicken and . . . and Pa gets us some furniture built, we can set a table to enjoy it."

Later that afternoon old Mrs. Tutchstone came slowly up the road with a sack in her hand. "These here are peas, Miz Stewart. Eat a few of 'em and plant the rest. It might not be too late for a batch before winter sets in."

Lizzie went out as soon as the old woman left and chopped up a little patch of earth in one corner of the field. She sent Synthia Catherine back to the creek with the pitcher for water, and then she mounded up two neat, short rows of the peas. "The start of our new garden," she said with satisfaction as she brushed the thick clay from her palms and the caked knee spots on her skirt.

An hour later Synthia Catherine rushed around the corner of the house when she heard her mother screeching at the top of her lungs. Lizzie was flapping her apron at an old hen who took refuge on top of a brush pile Walter created that morning at the edge of the field. "You wretched old hen, how dare you!" Lizzie was screaming. "We've got enough problems without you scratching up these rows of peas the minute I plant them. Walter! Walter! Come chase this horrid bird away from here!"

Walter came running around the other side of the house. "Chase her away? Lizzie, are you crazy? That horrid old bird might be a bit tough, but she'll make us a better dinner than we've had recently. Several nights' dinner, as a matter of fact."

Lizzie stopped screeching at the hen and smoothed her apron. "Oh," she said with a blank look. And then she began to laugh. "Well, catch her then, and unpack that iron pot we got in Chattanooga. I'm so tired and frustrated, I can't even recognize dinner when it struts right into my garden. You get the pot, and I'll replant as many of these peas as I can."

Sarah Stewart had just turned thirteen when the family returned to Sweetwater Creek. Perhaps her health was weakened by the dampness, filth, and poor food and water she had endured in the refugee prison in Louisville. Those conditions made her more vulnerable to illness than other children her age, and her nagging cough never completely disappeared, even after their return home.

On a chilly afternoon late in October, Sarah was caught outside in the field by a sudden, blinding rainstorm that soaked her through to the skin. She ran for the house, where Lizzie stripped her down in front of a roaring fire and wrapped her tightly in quilts. None of those precautions were any use. The dreaded rattling settled into Sarah's chest, and her fever mounted.

Just a month and two days after her thirteenth birthday, Sarah drew her last struggling breath and was laid to rest beside her little brother Jeff Davis Stewart. "I'm only glad we got her home first," sobbed Lizzie. "I couldn't have stood it if I'd had to leave one of my own up there in that awful place. Poor thing. She went through all those terrible experiences without a scratch, and then here at home she catches a cold she can't handle."

The rest of the year was hard, scraping food and wood together to go on living. They grieved every day over the loss of Sarah. Looking forward was barely possible, and yet it had to be done. The peas came up after Lizzie's second planting in time for a few meals, and Walter brought what he could from Atlanta, where he walked each week to do whatever work he could find. No more old hens strutted into the garden.

"At least we're all together," Lizzie repeated like a dull motto almost every morning. "Even Jeff Davis and Sarah. At least we're all together."

The rains came early in the spring. The house leaked terribly, but they kept the fire going in what was left of the stone fireplace. The rains created a swamp of rusty mud and kept everyone inside for days on end. Lizzie wouldn't let any of her three remaining children outside for more than a second or two. "Only when the sun is out full," she insisted.

When Synthia Catherine finally ventured out with Linnie Isabella one blue-sky morning in late March 1866, their feet made sucking sounds in the cool, thick mud. The sun was just coming up, and there was a cool breeze. "Let's go plant some more of Mama's peas," said Linnie Isabella.

"It's too early," said Synthia Catherine. "You can't plant peas yet. We still might get a frost."

But Linnie Isabella was already at the edge of the field and clapping her little hands. "Something's coming up," she called out. "Come and see. There's little green things all over."

Synthia Catherine squished and slipped to the edge of the field. Only a few brown vines remained where Lizzie had planted peas in the fall, but green shoots were poking through all over the rest of the field.

"Look, Sister," said Linnie Isabella. "God did our planting so we'd have a crop our first summer back."

Synthia Catherine looked out over the field, trying to figure out what could possibly be growing there. She was not sure what the little green shoots were, but she knew they weren't weeds.

Days later, the Stewarts realized that strawberry plants were pushing up all over their field. Synthia Catherine, Little Jim, and

Walter and Lizzie Stewart moved to Alabama sometime after the war. Lizzie died in 1887 at the age of fifty-one, and Walter remarried in 1888. *(Portrait of Walter Washington Stewart, his second wife, Martha A. Taylor Coffman, and three of their four sons provided from a family history collection on file at Sweetwater Creek State Park)*

Linnie Isabella tended the strawberry fields while their father walked off to find work each day in Atlanta. "We had thousands and thousands of strawberries," Synthia Catherine told her grandson when she was ninety years old.

"We gathered them up and carried them to Atlanta and sold them for money to live on, along with what Pa was making there. And then, after that first year, we never did have any strawberries come up anymore. That was God's work, you know. He gave us those strawberries as holy manna to eat and sell when we didn't have anything else. It was just obliged to have been that way, I guess, and Papa knew it was because he read it to us from the Good Book, there on the train when we were coming home."

THE ROSWELL EPILOGUE

After a short courtship, Mary Kendley married Albert Alexander May on July 20, 1865. The marriage took place almost exactly one year after she was forced to leave her life in Roswell.

Albert May was also a southerner who was uprooted and moved far from home. His parents married in Bulloch County, Georgia, in 1824 and moved south of Tallahassee to St. Marks, Florida, to operate a grocery store.

Albert fought for the Confederacy as a member of the Fourth Florida Infantry of Franklin County and was captured by Union

Albert May and Mary Kendley were married in Perry County, Indiana, on July 20, 1865, by Justice of the Peace John Bickler. *(Certified copy of marriage record used with permission of the Perry County (Indiana) Clerk's Office)*

forces near Jackson, Mississippi, in July 1863. He spent more than a year at Camp Morgan, a prisoner-of-war camp set up on the Indiana State Fairgrounds in Indianapolis—a camp not unlike Camp Chase in Columbus, Ohio, where Walter Washington Stewart endured nine months of hardship. Albert May was paroled on February 17, 1865, after signing an oath of allegiance to the U.S. government and promising to remain in the North as a loyal citizen.

Sometime after his parole, Albert arrived in Cannelton. When Mary Kendley first met Albert—perhaps on the street that June 1865 evening when she encountered one of Sherman's raiders—he had already found a job at Clark Brothers Pottery. Later he followed in his father's footsteps and opened a grocery store. Albert also worked as an agent for Howell Machine Company and then for Indiana Cotton Mills from 1881 until 1894.

After 1894 Albert May turned his interests to civil service. He won an appointment as Cannelton's postmaster under

Mary Kendley May and Albert May lived most of their adult lives in this narrow, two-story, sandstone-and-brick home on Fifth Street in Cannelton, Indiana. *(Photo by Barney Cook)*

Albert Alexander May, seated on left, and Mary Kendley May, seated on right, remained in Cannelton, Indiana, and had eight children. Their five sons who lived to adulthood were Walter Mark May, Albert Alexander May Jr., Thomas Hugh May, William Edward May, and John Raymond May. Their great-granddaughter, Mary Ida Robson Powers, directs a senior citizen center just two blocks from the family home where this family portrait was taken in the late 1890s. *(Family portrait used with permission of George and Elizabeth Kendley of Marietta, Georgia)*

President Grover Cleveland and was twice elected recorder for Perry County on the Democratic ticket. He also served two terms as a trustee of the local public schools. When Albert died at home in 1919, the *Cannelton Telephone* described him as a citizen "well and favorably known by all our people and up until his last illness was seen almost daily on our streets."

Mary Kendley married Albert May just two days after her twenty-second birthday. The narrow, two-story, sandstone-and-brick house where the couple lived most of their married life still stands on Fifth Street in Cannelton but is now abandoned and covered with vines. The Mays had eight children and outlived their parents.

When Mary Kendley May died in 1924, her obituary in the *Cannelton Telephone* mentioned her long-ago memories of Roswell, stating that she had once "heard the roar of the cannon in the Civil War" and was "at the edge of the battlefield when she lived in the South." The newspaper described her as a "great home woman who took great pride and interest in raising her family."

Sara Jane Kendley was twenty-nine years old in the spring of 1865 when her younger sister Mary married Albert May. Sara Jane did not marry until May 1870, but when she did, she also married a southerner—Andrew Jackson Nichols, a native of Bowling Green, Kentucky, whose parents were born in Virginia.

The May family headstone in Cliff Cemetery. *(Photo by Barney Cook)*

Thomas Hugh Kendley was sent north to Indiana with his brother and two sisters when he was seventeen. After the war, he found employment at the Indiana Cotton Mills facility in Cannelton, where he worked for forty-nine years. He died in 1915, "an old and highly respected bachelor and citizen" who lived at Cannelton's Cunningham Hotel. *(Family portrait of Thomas Hugh Kendley used with permission of George and Elizabeth Kendley of Marietta, Georgia)*

Mary Kendley May celebrated her twenty-first birthday in the back of a Union army wagon en route to Marietta, Georgia, from her home in Roswell. When she died in 1924, the *Cannelton Telephone* recalled that she had "once heard the roar of the cannon in the Civil War" and lived "at the edge of the battlefield when she lived in the South." *(Family portrait of Mary Kendley May used with permission of George and Elizabeth Kendley of Marietta, Georgia)*

Like Albert May, Andrew Nichols came to Cannelton in 1865 looking for work, perhaps after serving in the Confederate Army and being paroled by the Union. Like Albert, he went to work for Clark Brothers Pottery and was still employed by the company when he married Sara Jane.

Andrew had three children from a previous marriage, and census records suggest that his first wife died after he came to Cannelton, perhaps during the birth of their third child in 1868. Andrew and Sara Jane had one child, a daughter named Annie, who was born in 1877.

In 1909, Andrew and Sara Jane became seriously ill and moved to the home of Annie and her husband, John Sapp, in nearby Tell City, Indiana. Andrew died that year, and Sara Jane followed him in 1912. Her obituary described her as a pioneer citizen of Cannelton.

When Sara Jane Kendley married Andrew Nichols in 1870, her two younger brothers were still unmarried and were living with Albert and Mary Kendley May. Both twenty-three-year-old Thomas Hugh and twenty-year-old George worked for the Indiana Cotton Mills company at the time.

Thomas Hugh Kendley remained a confirmed bachelor all his life. He worked for Indiana Cotton Mills for forty-nine years and died "an old and highly respected bachelor and citizen" in 1915 while living at Cannelton's Cunningham Hotel.

George left his sister Mary's household in 1873 to marry Lucetta Johnson, a young woman from Ohio who came to Cannelton with her parents in 1859. George and Lucetta had three children, but only their daughter Olive lived to maturity.

In the early 1900s George retired from the cotton mill after more than fifty years of continuous service, but he continued to care for his poultry farm near Castlebury Creek. After Lucetta died in 1923, George moved to his daughter's home in Evansville. When

The May and Kendley family plots are just across the road from each other in Cliff Cemetery. The cemetery sits on a hill offering a view of the twin towers of the cotton mill and the wide Ohio River. *(Photos by Barney Cook)*

George died in 1930 he had outlived all of the brothers and sisters who came north from Roswell, as well as all of their spouses. The local newspaper described George as "a quiet, gentle, and unassuming man as well as an exemplary citizen."

Albert and Mary Kendley May's great-granddaughter Mary Ida Robson Powers was born in 1926. Although she never knew Albert and Mary, she knew their son Albert Jr. and his wife, Ida Gruver, who were her grandparents. Mary Ida was just a little girl when one of her aunts took her and the other great-grandchildren down to Albert and Mary Kendley May's home on Fifth Street to choose something of theirs as a keepsake before the house was closed up. Mary Ida chose a pair of small vases that she still has in her home.

Mary Ida chuckles when she sees the newspaper clipping about a trip Albert and Mary Kendley May took to Kansas in 1873, apparently planning to settle out there with several other Cannelton families. The venture did not work out, and the Mays returned to

Cannelton the following year after a side trip to visit family in Atlanta—probably Mary's older sister Matilda Anderson and her older brother John Robert Kendley, neither of whom was sent north during the war.

"You know what really happened out there?" Mary Ida asked while sipping coffee one morning at the senior citizen center she directs. The center occupies a converted house just one block over on Fifth Street from the vine-hidden house once owned by Albert and Mary May. "They made that trip to Kansas when my grandfather was a child," says Mary Ida. "They went by covered wagon and took all their little children with them.

"Apparently when they got out there, they fell in with a really rough group of people. In fact the group may have been outlaws. Anyway the story goes that they were going to arrest my greatgrandfather and maybe even hang him, but someone in the crowd recognized his Masonic lodge pin and rescued him." When the Mays returned to Cannelton in February 1874 the local newspaper announced that Albert May had decided to "remain satisfied that all is not gold that glitters and that distance lends enchantment to the view."

Mary Ida also remembers the family story about Mary Kendley spotting one of Sherman's soldiers on the street in Cannelton. "I don't remember what happened or anything, but I remember hearing about that. She recognized him as one of Sherman's soldiers from their march through Atlanta."

Mary Ida sorts through folders of genealogical information spread across a table in the senior citizen center's dining room. She was fascinated when she learned that Albert May's father, Robert, was an Irish child stolen and sent to sea as a cabin boy. He served on a merchant ship and spent time in prison in Russia when England was at war with that country. He was impressed into the British Navy on the high seas, jumped ship in Virginia, and settled in Rhode Island before heading south to Savannah.

Mary Ida describes the location of the Kendley and May plots in the quiet, tree-studded cemetery high up on the hill above Cannelton. "You just turn in at the main gate, and the Mays are all right up by the second road to the right. The Kendleys are buried just across the road."

On the winding drive up past St. Michael's Catholic Church and around to Cliff Cemetery and several other cemeteries, it is easy to catch a glimpse of the red tin roof and the twin towers of the Cannelton cotton mill and the pottery company that brought Mary Kendley and Albert May to this town. The buildings appear tiny in the distance from the cemetery road. Just beyond them flows the wide Ohio River, and just across the river lies Hawesville, Kentucky.

Margaret May Schank is also a descendant of Albert and Mary Kendley May. Her father, Walter Mark May, was a brother of Mary Ida's mother and also a son of Albert Jr. and Ida Gruver. Margaret has an excellent black-and-white photograph of Albert and Mary Kendley May with their children and grandchildren posed outside their Fifth Street Cannelton home, perhaps around 1900. She also has a framed portrait of the couple from a few years earlier—Albert with his thick, white, walrus mustache and Mary with her hair parted down the middle and pulled back severely into a bun.

Margaret Schank and her older sister, Irene May Dunlevy, have kept up with family genealogy by making charts and preserving files of letters and documents. They have shared their information with their younger brother, Harold, who is a foreman at Schwab Corporation in Cannelton. Margaret remembers Shirley Sapp, the great-granddaughter of Sara Jane Kendley Nichols, from school but does not know much about the family connection.

Margaret worked as a secretary at Cannelton High School for thirty years, and she has carefully preserved lists of all the graduating classes from that school, beginning with the very first one in 1897. George and Lucetta Kendley's daughter Olive and Albert and Mary May's son John Raymond were members of the 1897 class. Margaret proudly notes that her great-grandfather was serving as a member of the schoolboard at that time.

"I was in junior high when the cotton mill closed," says Margaret. "I have lived here all fifty-five years of my life, and that cotton mill was always the heart of things." She remembers that Shirley Sapp's family lived "down in the blocks"—the cotton mill blocks that were extremely similar to the millworker apartments in Roswell, Georgia. "I remember going down there as a child to play. They had a living room and a kitchen on the ground floor and a stairway up to the bedrooms. They were all connected on the block between Taylor and Fourth Street and Fifth and Main. The front doors faced the street on each side, and there was a big open area—Scrap Alley, some called it—in the back."

Memories fade with succeeding generations. Although Mary Ida Powers and Margaret May Schank have preserved some family stories about their ancestors coming to Cannelton from the South, they are only vaguely aware of the strong family connection between the May and Nichols families. They are not acquainted with any descendants of George and Lucetta Kendley, although the Kendleys and the Mays are buried directly across from each other in Cliff Cemetery. They know that the arrival of their ancestors in Cannelton was connected to General Sherman, but they picture Sherman's attack in terms of the larger city of Atlanta and know very little of Roswell or the events surrounding the burning of the mill buildings there in 1864.

Sara Jane Kendley Nichols elaborated the Roswell story for her daughter, Annie, as the years passed. Annie grew up in Cannelton and Tell City, Indiana, and except for a few years at a tobacco factory, worked all her adult life at the cotton mill as a speeder who turned yarn into thread, and as a slubber on the draw frame. Annie retired on a well-earned annuity just before World War II but returned to the mill a short time later to help with the war effort.

In March 1943 an article about her patriotic service appeared in the *Cannelton Telephone* under the headline "Patriotism and love for her work prompts Cannelton woman to continue in mill here." Annie Nichols Sapp told the reporter she had worked so long that she felt better when she was busy. She also understood the great military need for mill products.

That same article explained that war meant a great deal to Annie Sapp, because she remembered her mother's stories about escaping Atlanta when Union soldiers burned the city and tore up the tracks. The wonderful evolution of family legend is apparent in this newspaper clipping, which quotes Annie as stating that her mother, Sara Jane Kendley Nichols, was the last person to leave Atlanta before the city was leveled.

Annie's granddaughter Shirley Sapp lives in Indianapolis and works a full-time job while managing a theater. Shirley grew up in Cannelton and lived part of her childhood in "the blocks" apartments where the Kendley brothers and sisters most certainly lived when they first came to town to work at Indiana Cotton Mills.

One of Shirley's memories of growing up in Cannelton is riding the ferry across the Ohio River to Hawesville. It cost a quarter, but Shirley and her friends never paid because they never got off on the Hawesville side. They just rode back and forth all day for free. Shirley's grandmother told her that Sara Jane Kendley came right up the river to Hawesville on the train from Louisville and crossed the river there. This does not coincide with the records of other Kendley family members who clearly stated that they came to Cannelton from Indianapolis. But it is certainly the way Annie Sapp explained it to her granddaughter. "There's always been a ferry at Hawesville," says Shirley. "It was there until they built the bridge when the flood wall went up."

Shirley also is only vaguely familiar with the connection between her grandmother's family and the other Kendley sister and brothers who came to Cannelton in 1865. "I remember being told through the years that we were related to the Mays, but I've never done the genealogy to figure out that part of it," she says. "I was in the same class with Irene May Dunlevy, but we never really talked about that. And I knew Margaret May Schank was Irene's younger sister."

Shirley does remember her grandmother's wonderful stories about the Civil War. "She said Sherman killed many of the men who worked in the mill, but he got the women and children out of there. He sent the women away on the trains. There were a lot of eight- and nine-year-olds on that train. I remember her saying that. She also told me Sherman used the men to dig ditches and do other manual labor around Atlanta."

Shirley was about thirteen when Sara Jane Kendley Nichols died. "My grandmother's stories were, to me, like a drama, like something right out of a movie," she says. "I could just picture all those little girls being loaded on those trains. When I saw *Gone with the Wind,* I thought my family was a part of that in a small way."

In the 1980s Shirley lived in Arizona for a while and worked for the state government. On her lunch hours she went down to the state library and did research about Roswell, Georgia, in 1864 and 1865. She can't find her notes now, but she remembers one section she read that mentioned the "Roswell girls" coming to southern Indiana. The section talked about how brave they were, how the older ones took charge, held everybody together, and took care of the younger ones on the train and made sure they were okay. "You know," she says, "if you think about it, that must have been a terrible experience, being put on those trains and sent to somewhere so far away from everything you knew. It was a terrible thing they went through down there."

Although Mary Kendley visited her Georgia relatives at least twice after the Civil War, the connection between the Kendley descendants in Indiana and those in Georgia dwindled to nothing over the next hundred years. By the second half of the twentieth century, they lost all contact and had no particular awareness of each other. Although there was a great deal of interest in history about both places, very little of it focused on the millworkers.

In Roswell, the antebellum homes of the planter families were carefully preserved and several efforts were launched to determine the exact location of the original cotton mill. The later mill installations turned into shopping and restaurant concerns, and a visitor center opened. Most of Roswell's twentieth-century citizens who were aware that Sherman ordered several hundred millworkers sent north in 1864 simply viewed the refugees' fate as a mystery that would never be solved. But researcher Michael Hitt has carefully tracked the Roswell millworker story in his book, *Charged with Treason,* published in 1992. Hitt's book offers a chronological record of the Yankee invasion of Roswell and its aftermath.

Residents of Cannelton, Indiana, founded Historic Cannelton Inc., and successfully worked to have the mill placed on the National Register of Historic Places. Efforts are continuing to find a way to restore the mill that dominates the skyline of the town. Stories circulate in Cannelton about Union uniforms being made in the mill during the Civil War and about sandstone houses that might have harbored slaves on the Underground Railroad. But few stories have surfaced about the Georgia millworkers.

In 1974 George Kendley of Marietta, Georgia, received a letter from Hazel Litherland in Cannelton, Indiana. Hazel explained that her grandfather, Walter Mark May, was the second child of Albert and Mary Kendley May. Hazel concluded that George was her third cousin, and she was seeking information about John Wesley and Mary Evans Kendley. Hazel knew that two sisters and two brothers from Georgia set out for Indiana in 1864, but had no idea why. She happened to search for Kendleys in Cobb County, Georgia, because she had a copy of the letter Albert May's sister wrote to him during his visit to Roswell in 1873.

"Do you have any knowledge of this family?" Hazel Litherland asked George Kendley. "Are you perhaps a descendant of the same Mary and John Wesley Kendley? Do you know when and where they died and where they are buried?"

George Kendley of Marietta, Georgia, continues to search for the answer to that last question. He still has no idea where the parents of Sara Jane and Mary, Thomas Hugh and George Kendley are buried. He still has no idea what happened to the other siblings, Catherine and Elizabeth and William. But the correspondence that he and Hazel Litherland carried on for a decade filled in many gaps in family history for both of them. They exchanged family tree charts, copies of property deeds, newspaper clippings, and other documents.

George Kendley finds the story Mary Ida Powers tells about the Masonic lodge pin and the rescue of Albert May in Kansas particularly interesting. His own great-grandfather, John Robert Kendley, was also a Mason. John Robert, the older brother of the four Kendleys who were sent north, moved to Smyrna, Georgia, after the Civil War and worked in the Ruff Mill near the covered bridge over Nickajack Creek. "John Robert Kendley used to walk up to Marietta every week with his buddies for Masonic meetings," says George. "Everybody was dirt-poor then, after the war. They decided to start a Masonic lodge in Smyrna, and John Robert was the first Worshipful Master there."

George Kendley continues to search for links in the history of his family, hoping to find out what happened to his great-great-grandparents and their missing children. He thinks it is possible that Catherine and Elizabeth died during the trip north to Louisville, but he has no proof of that. Recently he made a trip to New England to visit some Kendleys there. Before leaving he packed up his files and photographs and stories so he could share what he knows and perhaps add a little more to his own collection from someone else's family lore.

Not all of the Roswell millworkers found their way to Cannelton, Indiana, but the Kendleys were certainly not the only ones who did. Of the forty-eight Georgia-born cotton millworkers employed by the Indiana Cotton Mills in 1870, at least thirty of them can be traced, along with other family members, directly back to the mills of Roswell, Georgia, in 1860.

Elizabeth James and her daughter Sarah were among those arrested in Roswell. By 1870 Elizabeth was a sixty-five-year-old widow living in Cannelton, and Sarah was working at the cotton mill and had married a farmhand from Tennessee named Noah Swallow.

The entire Fretwell family came to Indiana from Roswell, and all of them were still together there in 1870. We can only imagine how difficult that journey must have been for Lavina Fretwell, traveling with six daughters ranging in age from seven to twenty-three. Lavina's husband, Littleton, was a member of the Roswell Battalion and either traveled with her or joined her later. Their son Isaac deserted the battalion, surrendered to Union troops, and probably rejoined the family in either Louisville or Cannelton. By 1870 he married a woman named Nancy who may have been from Roswell. Both worked at Indiana Cotton Mills in Cannelton.

Lively (Elirly) Moore also made the journey north with part of her family. Robert was eleven and Tocoa (Cora) was ten when the Yankees came to Roswell. After the war Robert became a chair maker in Cannelton. His sister worked at the cotton mill until her marriage in 1874 to Samuel Morrison Conner. Lively Moore's older son John served with the Roswell Battalion and came to Cannelton during or after the war. He married Mary A. Hopkins of Roswell and brought her mother, Cynthia, to live with them. Both John and Mary worked at Indiana Cotton Mills in 1870.

It is extremely difficult to trace young single or widowed girls who worked in the Roswell mill and made the journey north, because most of them married (or married again), taking their husbands' names after reaching Indiana. Unless other family members came with them or they remained single, it is hard to link them to the Roswell census records.

One young millworker who can be traced is Georgianna Morgan, who was seventeen when the census was taken in Roswell in 1860. She worked in the mill and was married to Alex Morgan, a young wagoner for Roswell Manufacturing Company. Georgianna was arrested in 1864 and traveled north with their two children, four-year-old William and two-year-old Lula. By 1870 she was a young widow living with her two children in Cannelton and working at Indiana Cotton Mills.

Pleasant Bryan(t) and his oldest son, Augustus Franklin Bryan, served in the Roswell Battalion during the Civil War. Pleasant and his wife, Nancy, along with the rest of the Bryan(t) family made their way to Cannelton from Indianapolis in 1868. Their descendants were still living and working there in 1943.

Many of the Roswell families sent north did not stay there. The daughters of Margarette Wood (the woman who reportedly died in a chair in Louisville) settled in Kentucky for a while. Easter Wood married a man named Merritt and had two children, but died at a young age and was buried in Louisville. There is no record of Molly Ann Wood's adult life except family notes that suggest she lived until 1893.

Lucinda Elizabeth Wood married James Williamson Shelly of Montgomery, Alabama, in December 1866. Shelly served in the Alabama infantry and spent time in a Yankee prison in Alton, Illinois. He took the oath of allegiance at Chattanooga in August 1864 and met Lucinda in Louisville after her journey from Roswell. Lucinda and James had nine children and lived in Effingham, Illinois, until 1886 when they returned to Georgia. Both Lucinda and James are buried in the Zion Hill Baptist Church cemetery near Cartersville.

Samuel and Rebecca Jane Farr were among the millworkers who returned to Roswell. In *Charged with Treason,* Michael Hitt states that Samuel Farr found employment in Indianapolis, but at some point after the war, returned to Roswell with Rebecca and Jonathan.

No records indicate whether Samuel's parents made the journey to Indianapolis. If they did, they also returned to Georgia. Samuel's father, Jonathan Farr, worked as a watchman for Roswell

Manufacturing Company before the war. When he died in 1895, he was buried in the Methodist cemetery in Roswell. His wife, Jane, was buried next to him in 1898.

It is probable that Samuel Farr returned to work at the mill in Roswell. Barrington King wrote a letter to his son Ralph on July 22, 1865, mentioning that some of the families sent north were returning by that time. "Everyone around seems to feel the loss sustained by destruction of the mills and are anxious that we rebuild," wrote Barrington. He also mentioned that returning soldiers were "anxious to work at sixty cents a day and appear very orderly."

That orderliness was quite a contrast to the disorder and destruction Barrington King remembered from the previous July just after the Yankee invasion. He mentioned it in a statement he made at the first post-war stockholders meeting of Roswell Manufacturing Company. "We regret much to report the conduct of a few men, in our employment for years with the women and children, from whom we expected protection from [sic] our property—they plundered & destroyed to a large amount, tearing down the shelves in the store to burn, breaking glasses, and otherwise injuring the houses, hauling off iron and copper to sell and putting the wheel in motion and seriously injuring it by throwing down rocks."

Whatever damage was done didn't stop the mill from reopening. Samuel Farr returned to work there and lived to the age of seventy-seven. He was buried in the Roswell Methodist Cemetery in 1913. Rebecca Jane was buried next to her husband in 1926.

Their son Jonathan Davis Farr, who fell from the Union Army wagon on the way to Indiana in 1865, was still working at Mill No. 2 in Roswell in 1893 after he was promoted to boss in March 1891.

Some descendants of Samuel and Rebecca Jane Farr now live in Charlotte, North Carolina. Their son Jonathan had at least two children, including a son named Hugh who often told the story about how his father fell from the wagon and how the deep mud saved him from getting crushed to death. Hugh also gave one of his nieces a gold wedding band she believes belonged to Rebecca Jane Whitmire Farr, Samuel's wife.

In addition to the Farrs, some supervisory personnel from the mills returned to Roswell after the war. Olney Eldridge traveled as far north as Louisville but came back and was again employed by Roswell Manufacturing Company. Theodore Adams also returned after his wife died in Cincinnati in August 1864 during her attempted trip to New York.

It is difficult to trace the fate of each and every millworker and millworker family member sent north from Roswell. An 1866 military report issued by Brevet Brigadier-General D. C. McCallum reveals at least one factor that contributes to the lack of existing information about the millworkers. "No record was kept of the contrabands, refugees, and rebel deserters that poured back of active operations," wrote McCallum. "General Sherman ordered all sent to the rear who could not feed themselves, and they were placed upon the first train going in the direction by post commanders."

Widows and young girls changed their names after marriage, and many people headed west after the war during a time when records were sketchy in frontier areas. The sketchy records increase the difficulty of finding information about the millworker refugees. We do know that at least thirty people from Roswell, Georgia, settled in Cannelton, Indiana, and that many others eventually made their way back to Georgia. William Gilbert was a machinist at a Roswell mill before the war and was sent north with his wife, C. H. Gilbert, and two children. They returned in 1866 and made their home in Jewell, Georgia. John and Mary Brown went to Indianapolis but returned to Atlanta in the late 1870s.

A list of Roswell Mill No. 2 employees extracted from an original ledger for May 1890 through December 1893 shows a number of family names that match names of employees who worked in the mill at the time of the Civil War. The ledger information suggests that members of the Ashley, Bell, Brown, Bush, Findley, Frazer, Hicks, Kirk, Mullins, Parks, Roberson, Sampler, and Voss families did not disappear from Roswell entirely as a result of the war.

A list of Civil War veterans living in Cobb County, Georgia, in 1906 offers another clue to millworkers and their families who returned to or never left the Roswell area. The veterans listed who were former millworkers include W. A. Camp, W. S. Dodgen, M. E. Dodgen, George Downs, William Dupree, Pinkney Fields, L. E. Fowler, Daniel Hopkins, John Hunter, J. M. Kirk, John R. Kinley (Kendley), S. J. Lindsey, A. S. Mitchell, B. W. Osburn, and E. P. Paden.

In addition, numerous family names of female millworkers from 1860 match family names on this 1906 veterans list, suggesting that the wives and children of these veterans also returned to or never left Roswell. The names listed include Bagwell, Bell, Brown, Butler, Coleman, Cox, Hendrix, Hopkins, James, Moore, Moss, Mullins, Norton, Owens, Reed, and Sherman.

Although these lists of names are not tied to specific family stories or written records, they do suggest again that the Roswell millworkers General Sherman arrested did not disappear entirely after their ordeal during the war. To be sure, these refugees had a difficult time and their lives were forever changed. But after the war, a large number of them picked up the pieces and went on with their lives where they found themselves after the war or after returning home to Roswell.

THE SWEETWATER
EPILOGUE

The owners of the Sweetwater Creek mill did not rebuild after the Civil War. All that remains is a faded remnant brooding in eerie silence among the trees next to the limestone shoals. What was left of the town of New Manchester (Factory Town) has settled deeper and deeper into a carpet of rust-colored pine needles and leaves. Only recently has excavation begun to re-create the pathways of the small milltown where Synthia Catherine and others lived on the night they watched the meteor shower and on the morning they spotted the blue-coated Yankees marching along the creek bank toward their mill.

The half-mile (one-way) History Trail at Sweetwater Creek State Park is not strenuous. Hikers who follow its red markers can follow the "main street" of the Civil War–era town of New Manchester and view the mill ruins, the site of the town store, and the mill race. *(Photo by Barney Cook)*

Hikers who visit the ruins of the cotton mill at Sweetwater Creek can stand on the modern bridge above the creek and see the rock-lined mill race immediately downstream. It was built with manual labor and had a series of gates to control water flow to the mill. *(Photo by Barney Cook)*

The Stewart family had a difficult time accepting that their oldest child, Sarah E. Stewart, survived so many hardships during the war and then could not overcome a chill in a rainstorm after she finally made it home. Sarah died at age thirteen on October 20, 1865, after the family finally completed their journey all the way back to Georgia.

Synthia Catherine's younger brother and sister, who also made the journey to Louisville and back, did not live long lives. Little Jim (James Buchanan Stewart) died in 1895 at age thirty-eight. He married twice but had no children. Linnie Isabella married young, like her mother, at age fifteen, to John T. King. She died in 1884 at age twenty-five.

Lizzie and Walter Stewart had two more children after the Civil War. Mary Elizabeth was born in May 1866 and died in 1890. Robert Allen was born in August 1868 and died in 1931. According to family historian Lucille Stewart Jones of Stephenville, Texas, the family did not remain in the Sweetwater Creek area. They moved to DeKalb County in northeast Alabama, where Lizzie died in 1887 at the age of fifty-one. According to Lucille, Walter married again and had four additional sons. He lived until 1904 and is buried in Old Mount Vernon Cemetery on Lookout Mountain near Collbran, Alabama.

Synthia Catherine married Ephraim David Bass Boyd, from Smyrna, Georgia, in January 1878. The wedding reportedly took place at Walter and Lizzie's home in Gaylesville in northeast Alabama with about a hundred guests attending. Synthia Catherine and David had nine children of their own and also raised six of David's brothers and sisters when David's parents died shortly after Synthia Catherine and David married. After Lizzie Stewart died, Synthia Catherine and David looked after Synthia's younger brothers and sisters for about a year until her father, Walter, remarried in late 1888.

Synthia Catherine and David moved to Comanche County, Texas, in 1903, and lived in Indian Creek and "on the Huff Ranch" before settling permanently near Sidney. David died in 1928 at age seventy-eight, but Synthia Catherine lived on in Sidney for another twenty-six years. She was known to friends and relatives as "Grannie Boyd" until her death in 1954.

In 1947, when she was ninety-two, Synthia Catherine made a 78-rpm recording with her grandson Archie Grady Elwood Boyd Jr. On that recording she told a number of stories about her life in Sweetwater Creek, her family's arrest by the Yankees, and their shipment by train through Marietta to Louisville. She talked about the family reunion before Walter was sent to Camp Chase, and the family's eventual return to Georgia. Synthia Catherine Stewart Boyd's memories represent one of a few personal accounts of this Civil War trail of tears drama. The stories she told on the recording coincide directly with dates and events that can be documented in other sources.

Synthia Catherine may have embellished her Civil War stories in the last few years of her life, or perhaps her relatives and newspaper reporters added the flourishes. For whatever reason, her obituary in a Comanche County newspaper erroneously suggested that Synthia Catherine lived on Peach Street in

Synthia Catherine Stewart, third from left in this family portrait taken after 1903, married Ephraim David Bass Boyd, second from left, in January 1878. *(Portrait provided from a family history collection on file at Sweetwater Creek State Park)*

Atlanta when that city was looted and burned by the Yankees. The obituary also suggested that Synthia Catherine and her family crossed a bridge and got out of Atlanta just before the Yankees burned it. This same obituary stated that it was during this escape from Atlanta that Synthia Catherine grabbed the Bible that was stolen by a Yankee soldier and later restored to her by General Sherman himself.

One of the saddest stories from the Sweetwater Creek episode of the Civil War is that of A. J. and Margaret White. No specific record exists of Margaret and her children's confinement in Louisville during 1864 and 1865, but we do know that they were among the millworkers Sherman sent north and that they returned to the Atlanta area after the war.

The only war record available for A. J. White indicates that he transferred from his original infantry battalion to the Sixty-fifth Regiment of the Georgia Infantry in March 1863, almost a year after he wrote the one letter from Savannah that remains of his correspondence with his wife. One source suggests that A. J. White died in a Union prison camp, but another indicates that he assumed his wife and children remained in the North and searched for them there at the end of the war.

Perhaps like a woman named Eliza Hannon, A. J. White placed an advertisement in a Cincinnati or Louisville newspaper seeking information about Margaret. Eliza Hannon placed such an ad looking for her husband, Patrick, in a Cincinnati newspaper. She wanted her husband to know that she would be waiting for him in the Railroad Hotel in Louisville.

A. J. White never found Margaret and died before he could return to Georgia and discover that she made her way safely home to Sweetwater Creek. Confederate military records state that he died near Chattanooga, Tennessee, sometime after 1863. Staff members at Sweetwater Creek State Park were told that he died in southern Indiana while searching for his family, but no written records exist to prove this.

Existing Sweetwater Creek records do not indicate whether Margaret White married again, but one of her two children married into the Clay family, and Margaret later became the grandmother of General Lucius DuBignon Clay. General Clay is best known for directing the airlift of supplies to the Allied sectors of Berlin when they were cut off from the West by a Soviet blockade after World War II.

Henry Lovern, the young overseer of the cardroom at the Sweetwater Creek mill, did not make the journey north with the other millworkers. Confederate military records list him as a member of the Campbell Salt Springs Guards, the same unit

Walter Stewart and several others from Sweetwater Creek joined. It is possible that Lovern caught up with this unit when they were fighting in the Atlanta area after the Yankees burned the mill at Sweetwater Creek. Pension records indicate that Lovern surrendered to Union forces at High Point, North Carolina, on April 26, 1865.

In December 1867 Henry Lovern gave a court deposition in connection with a lawsuit about the Sweetwater Creek mill property. In that deposition he testified about the arrival of Union troops in Sweetwater Creek and the burning of the mill on July 9, 1864. He estimated that it would have taken 220 wagonloads to remove all the machinery from the mill (excluding the waterwheel) before the Yankees arrived.

The grandson of Nathaniel Humphries, W. A. Humphries, was ninety-one years old in 1986 when he told *The Atlanta Journal and Constitution* that he remembered visiting the mill ruins with his father when he was a teenager just after 1900. W. A. Humphries's father was the son of Nathaniel Humphries, who ran the company store at Sweetwater Creek before the war. The 1860 census for New Manchester (Sweetwater Creek) village lists a number of people with the last name Humphries, but it is not clear which ones were directly related to Nathaniel. The names include Amanda Humphries, the woman Synthia Catherine Stewart describes selling her homespun dress to a Yankee lady in Marietta. The list also includes John Benjamin Humphries and Wiley T. Humphries, who served in the Campbell Salt Springs Guards with Walter Stewart. John Benjamin Humphries was captured in Decatur, Alabama, on October 31, 1864, and released from Camp Douglas, Illinois, on May 13, 1865. Wiley T. Humphries was wounded at Perryville, Kentucky, on October 8, 1862, and died in Vicksburg in July 1863.

S. H. Causey, who made the journey north with his mother, his older brother who was in poor health, and several younger children, is the only Sweetwater Creek millworker who is known to have worked in Indianapolis during the final months of the Civil War. In 1932 Judge Lewis C. Russell interviewed Causey for an article in *The Atlanta Journal*. Russell was an uncle of Governor Richard B. Russell Jr., whose grandfather, William J. Russell, was one of the original owners of the Sweetwater Creek mill.

S. H. Causey, who was eighty-six years old in 1932, lived near Sweetwater Creek in Lithia Springs, just west of Atlanta. He told Russell his memories of working in the spinning room and watching the Yankees burn the mill in July 1864. Causey also described his mother's decision to take her chances on going north and the Federal officers granting her permission for her older son to come out of hiding and travel north with the family.

Causey clearly stated in his interview that he and other family members suffered greatly in Indiana during the intensely cold winter of 1864–65, but they did find employment in Indianapolis. They were the only family from Sweetwater Creek known to have done so. He also stated that his family returned south on the same train that took them north one year earlier, and that many other refugees also returned to their homes after the war.

There seems to be much more speculation about the fate of the millworkers from Sweetwater Creek than the fate of those from Roswell. This is due in large part to the fact that the owners of Roswell Manufacturing Company rebuilt its mills and provided jobs for returning refugees, while the owners of the Sweetwater Creek mill did not. For years newspaper and magazine articles have questioned the events at New Manchester (Factory Town) on Sweetwater Creek and implied a great unsolved mystery involving the refugees Sherman shipped north. Some articles have even suggested that none of the Georgia millworker families were ever heard from again.

A 1955 fire at the county courthouse in Douglasville, where many of the Sweetwater Creek records were stored, destroyed many documents, making it particularly difficult to verify the fate of the refugees. Unfortunately there was not enough historical interest in the area before the fire to warrant making copies of the records and storing them in another place. But existing church and family records certainly indicate that many of the Sweetwater Creek refugees made their way back to Georgia after the war.

Since the refugees who returned to Sweetwater Creek found no rebuilt mill or promise of other jobs, many of them probably moved on—most likely westward—soon after their return. Millworker William Garland Tackett, for example, moved to Arkansas in the 1870s and died there in 1917. Miles Nathaniel Mozley, a seventeen-year-old mill employee in 1863, died years later in Dallas, Texas.

Researcher Monroe King remains convinced that there was a Federal conspiracy to cover up the fate of the men who worked at the Sweetwater Creek mill. The Union troops separated the men from the women, and King wonders if perhaps at least some of the men were killed or shipped out of the country. He believes many of them simply disappeared and were never heard from again.

Confederate war records, however, suggest that many of the men who worked in the mill in 1860 were enlisted or conscripted into rebel military units by the time the Yankees reached Sweetwater Creek in the summer of 1864. And the few existing records include some documentation of families and individuals— such as the Causeys, Stewarts, Henry Lovern and Margaret White—who either never left Georgia or who left and returned after the war.

According to an abstract prepared by Joe Baggett of Douglasville, Georgia, forty-nine men of draft age were working in the Sweetwater Creek mill in December 1863, but no proof has been found of how many of them were still there the following July. We do know, however, that a fairly large percentage of those male workers were living and working in the same general vicinity after the Civil War ended.

Columbus Blair, for example, was a twenty-eight-year-old employee at the Sweetwater Creek mill in December 1863 and was not serving in the military at that time. After the war Blair worked as a fertilizer dealer, and in 1895 he served as a representative from Douglas County.

John C. Bowden, who was a forty-five-year-old employee at the Sweetwater Creek mill in 1863, had operated a store at Salt (Lithia) Springs at some time after 1850. He died in 1891 and was buried in Bowden-Mozley Cemetery in Lithia Springs. This record suggests what may have been true of many of the male employees at Sweetwater Creek—Bowden worked at the mill but did not live in New Manchester (Factory Town), and he had other business interests in addition to the mill.

William J. Croker, who was a thirty-seven-year-old employee at the Sweetwater Creek mill in 1863, died in 1898 and was buried at Union Grove Church near Lithia Springs. Croker's daughter married Obadiah C. Renfroe who, according to Confederate pension records, served as a guard at the Sweetwater Creek factory during the Civil War. Both Renfroe and his wife were buried at Union Grove Church.

The Tolbert family history includes a story about Martha Ann Tolbert, who reportedly got a job at the Sweetwater Creek mill at age twelve without her parents' knowledge. Instead of going to school she worked at the mill each day and was arrested by Union soldiers when she was sixteen. Her granddaughter, Fannie Lou Hendrix, told family historians that Martha Ann was put on a train with other millworkers and sent north to Ohio. She remained there until the end of the war when she returned to the Sweetwater Creek area. Martha Ann married Yancey Amos Boynton in the late 1860s and moved to Powder Springs, where she raised nine children.

The Jennings family also did not disappear after their forced journey north. In 1860 Gideon Jennings worked at the Sweetwater Creek mill and lived in the area with his wife, Jane Whitley Jennings, and their seven children, including one-year-old Elizabeth. Family records and an obituary indicate that the Jenningses were sent to Indiana by the Union military and stayed there until the Civil War ended. Elizabeth told family members later about the trip north, even describing stops along the way so that the women could prepare meals for their families beside the railroad tracks. When Elizabeth was seven, which would have been 1867, the Jennings family returned to the Sweetwater Creek area. Elizabeth later married James A. Young and lived in Whitesburg (Carroll County), Georgia, until she died at age ninety-three.

It is impossible to trace every millworker family sent north from Sweetwater Creek, because so few records were kept and very few of the records that were kept survived the 1955 courthouse fire. Even so, enough documentation exists to indicate that many who made the journey north from Sweetwater Creek survived and returned to Georgia after the war.

BIBLIOGRAPHY

"Aid for Refugees," *Louisville* (Kentucky) *Daily Journal,* 24 August 1864.

"Albert Alexander May," *Cannelton* (Indiana) *Telephone,* 18 February 1908.

"Alumni of Cannelton High School," *Cannelton* (Indiana) *Inquirer,* 21 April 1923.

"Arrival of Women and Children from the South," *Cincinnati* (Ohio) *Daily Commercial,* 25 July 1864.

Atlanta History Center Library Archives, Civil War Manuscript Collections, Atlanta, Georgia. King Family Papers—correspondence between Barrington S. King and his family and Barrington King Jr.'s application for leave in December 1863. *Diary and Personal Memorandum Book of Private James P. Snell, Co. A, 52d., Ill. Vol. Inft. at the Headquarters of the Second Division, Sixteenth Army Corps In the Field During the Summer and Fall of 1864.* Stewart Family Collection—transcript of Civil War oral history by Synthia Catherine Stewart Boyd. Walter Stewart Clan compiled by Lucille Stewart Jones.

"Brief History of Roswell, GA." www.ethom.com/roswell/history.

Bulloch Hall, Roswell, Georgia. Michael D. Hitt historical manuscript and research collections: Tolbert Family History. Notes on the Martha Freeman Wright Family. Roswell Methodist Church History. French and American Claims Commission Report, Theophile Roché *vs.* The United States, 1884-1885. Testimony of A. S. Atkinson & Others, Executors of the Estate of Charles McDonald Dec. *vs.* A. V. Brumby & W. J. Russell in May 1869 to the Superior Court of Fulton County, State of Georgia. Wood Family Papers.

Byrd Library Special Collections, Syracuse University, Syracuse, N. Y. Mary Walker Papers.

Cahill, Bill. Interview by author. Sweetwater Creek State Park, Lithia Springs, Georgia. March 1997.

Cannan, John. *The Atlanta Campaign: May-November, 1864.* Conshohocken, Pa.: Combined Books, Inc., 1991.

Cannelton (Indiana) *Economist,* 28 April 1849.

Cannelton (Indiana) *Inquirer,* 14 and 28 February 1874.

Castel, Albert E. *Decision in the West: The Atlanta Campaign of 1864.* Lawrence, Kans.: University Press of Kansas, 1992.

"The Chattahoochee River," *Cincinnati* (Ohio) *Daily Commercial,* 8 August 1864.

Cincinnati (Ohio) *Daily Commercial,* 18 July 1864; 4, 19, and 29 August 1864; 14 September 1864.

Collins, Lewis. *Collins' Historical Sketches of Kentucky; History of Kentucky.* Revised by Richard H. Collins. Covington, Ky: Collins & Co., 1882.

"Commemorative Book and 150th Anniversary Program." Cannelton, Ind.: Sesquicentennial, Inc., 1987.

Darbe, Leigh. Interview by author. Indiana Historical Society Library. 25 June 1997.

Dawsey, Cyrus B., and James M. Dawsey, ed. *The Confederados: Old South Immigrants in Brazil.* Tuscaloosa, Ala.: University of Alabama Press, 1995.

De la Hunt, Thomas James. *Perry County: A History.* Indianapolis: The W. K. Stewart Company, 1916.

Denney, Robert E. *Civil War Prisons & Escapes: A Day by Day Chronicle.* New York: Sterling Publishing Company, 1993.

"The Destitute Condition of Southern Refugees," *Louisville* (Kentucky) *Daily Journal,* 11 August 1864.

"Details of the Operation—Rebel Accounts," *Cincinnati* (Ohio) *Daily Commercial,* 19 July 1864.

Elkhorn (Wisconsin) *Independent,* 10 August 1864.

Fairley, Mrs. David. Telephone conversation with author. Charlotte, North Carolina. 4 February 1997.

Farr, Julia. Telephone conversation with author. Charlotte, North Carolina. 4 February 1997.

"The Female Military Prison in Louisville," *Cincinnati* (Ohio) *Daily Commercial,* 7 September 1864.

Foote, Shelby. *The Civil War: A Narrative.* New York: Random House, 1974.

"From Sherman's Army," *Cincinnati* (Ohio) *Daily Commercial,* 25 July 1864.

"General Order," *Louisville* (Kentucky) *Daily Journal,* 22 August 1864.

"General Sherman on Recruiting in the Rebel States," *Cincinnati* (Ohio) *Daily Commercial,* 18 August 1864.

Griggs, William Clark. *The Elusive Eden: Frank McMullan's Confederate Colony in Brazil.* Austin, Tex.: University of Texas Press, 1987.

Harter, Eugene C. *The Lost Colony of the Confederacy.* Jackson, Miss.: University Press of Mississippi, 1985.

"Headquarters District of Kentucky, General Orders No. 63," *Cincinnati* (Ohio) *Daily Commercial,* 18 August 1864.

"Historic Dahlonega, Georgia." web.infoave.net/"d...istory/histdahl.

History of Warrick, Spencer and Perry Counties, Indiana. Chicago: Goodspeed, Brothers & Co., 1885.

Hitt, Michael D. "Bulloch Hall." Roswell, Ga.: 1995.

————. *Charged With Treason.* Monroe, N.Y.: Library Research Associates, Inc., 1992.

Hitt, Michael D. Interview by author. Bulloch Hall, Roswell, Georgia. June 1997.

Hoehling, A. A. *Last Train from Atlanta.* New York: Thomas Yoseloff, 1958.

Howard, Frances Thomas. *In and Out of the Lines.* New York: The Neale Publishing Company, 1905.

"Important from Governor Brown of Georgia, A Proclamation," *Cincinnati* (Ohio) *Daily Commercial,* 27 July 1864.

"The Indiana Cotton Mills: An Experiment in North-South Cooperation." *Indiana History Bulletin* 42, no. 5 (May 1965).

Jackson, Olin, ed. *A North Georgia Journal of History.* Woodstock, Ga.: Legacy Communications, 1989.

Kemble, Frances Anne. *Journal of a Residence on a Georgian Plantation in 1838-1839.* Athens, Ga.: University of Georgia Press, 1984.

Kendley, George Howard. Interviews by author. Marietta, Georgia. 1996 and 1997.

Kennett, Lee B. *Marching through Georgia: The Story of Soldiers and Civilians during Sherman's Campaign.* New York: HarperCollins, 1995.

Key, William. *The Battle of Atlanta and the Georgia Campaign.* Atlanta: Peachtree Publishers, Ltd., 1981.

King, John H., M.D. *Three Hundred Days in a Yankee Prison: Reminiscences of War Life, Captivity, Imprisonment at Camp Chase, Ohio.* Kennesaw, Ga.: Continental Book Company, 1959.

King, Monroe Martin. "Destruction of New Manchester, Georgia: The Story behind the Ruins at Sweetwater Creek State Park." Douglasville, Ga.: 1982.

_____. Interview by author. Douglasville, Georgia. 9 October 1996.

King, Spencer Bidwell, Jr. *Ebb Tide: As Seen through the Diary of Josephine Clay Habersham, 1863.* Athens, Ga.: University of Georgia Press, 1958.

Lawson, Sherron D. *A Guide to the Historic Textile Mill Town of Roswell, Georgia.* Roswell, Ga.: The Roswell Historical Society, Inc., 1996.

Lilly Library, Indiana University, Bloomington, Indiana. Indiana Cotton Mills Papers.

Litherland, Hazel. Telephone conversation with author. Tell City, Indiana. 31 March 1997.

"Local Items," *Cannelton* (Indiana) *Reporter,* 8 October 1864, 17 and 23 December 1864; 3 May 1865; 20 and 27 July 1865; 21 September 1865.

Louisville (Kentucky) *Daily Journal,* 4 and 9 August 1864.

Louisville (Kentucky) *Daily Union Press,* 27 July 1864.

Lucas, Silas Emmet. *The 1832 Gold Lottery of Georgia: Containing a List of the Fortunate Drawers in Said Lottery.* Easley, S.C.: Southern Historical Press, 1976.

"Marietta, Georgia, History." www.peachweb.com/marietta/history.

Martin, Clarece. *Roswell: Historic Homes and Landmarks.* Roswell, Ga.: The Roswell Historical Society, Inc., 1974.

Massey, Mary Elizabeth. *Women in the Civil War.* Lincoln, Nebr: University of Nebraska Press, 1994.

Middleton, Lee. *Hearts of Fire: Soldier Women of the Civil War.* Torch, Ohio: Lee Middleton, 1993.

Mitchell, Broadus. *The Rise of Cotton Mills in the South.* Baltimore: The Johns Hopkins Press, 1921.

Myers, Robert Manson ed. *The Children of Pride: A True Story of Georgia and the Civil War.* New Haven, Conn.: Yale University Press, 1972.

Nashville (Tennessee) *Daily Press & Times,* 10 August 1864.

National Archives and Record Administration. Records of prisoners at Camp Morgan, Indianapolis, Indiana.

New Albany (Indiana) *Daily Ledger,* 8 October 186; 17 and 23 December 1864.

"A New Order from General Sherman—Paroled Prisoners and Refugees To Be Furnished Transportation to Interior Points," *Louisville* (Kentucky) *Daily Journal,* 19 August 1864.

The New York Commercial, 9 September 1864.

The New York Tribune, 21 July 1864—May 1865.

"North Georgia History." www.ngeorgia.com/history.

Obituary notice for Albert Alexander May, *Cannelton* (Indiana) *Telephone,* 27 March 1919.

Obituary notice for Andy Nichols, *Cannelton* (Indiana) *Telephone,* 14 January 1909.

Obituary notice for George W. Kendley, *Tell City* (Indiana) *News,* 7 June 1930.

Obituary notice for Mary Kendley May, *Cannelton* (Indiana) *Telephone,* 25 April 1924.

Obituary notice for Mrs. George (Lucetta Johnson) Kendley, *Cannelton* (Indiana) *Inquirer,* 21 March 1923.

"Old Citizen Passes Away," *Cannelton* (Indiana) *Inquirer,* 24 February 1912.

Old County Courthouse Museum, Cannelton, Indiana. Charles Poehlein and Michael F. Rutherford Research Records. Photographs and memorabilia of Cannelton families and businesses.

"Patriotism and Love for her work prompts Cannelton woman to continue in mill here," *Cannelton* (Indiana) *Telephone,* 19 March 1943.

Photographic History of the Civil War. New York: The Review of Reviews Company, 1911.

Poehlein, Chuck. Interview by author. Old Perry County Courthouse Museum, Cannelton, Indiana. 8 May 1997.

Powers, Mary Ida and Robert. Interview by author. Cannelton, Indiana. 7 May 1997.

Rare Book, Manuscript, and Special Collections Library, Duke University, Durham, North Carolina. Letter from Andrew J. White to Margaret White (13 June 1862) in Andrew J. White Mss.

Rawlinson, Mary Stewart, ed. *The Walter Stewart Family History.* Columbia, S.C.: The State Printing Company, 1982.

"The Rebel Press," *Cincinnati* (Ohio) *Daily Commercial,* 27 July 1864.

"Rebel Prisoners," *Louisville* (Kentucky) *Daily Journal,* 11 August 1864.

Rogers, Robert L. *An Historical Sketch of the Georgia Military Institute, Marietta, Georgia.* 1890. Reprint, Atlanta: Kimsey's Book Shop, 1956.

"Roswell Historical Society." www.ethom.com.roswell/histmone.

Roswell Historical Society Archives, Roswell, Georgia. Roswell Manufacturing Company History by Richard G. Coleman, 1982. Letter from Nathaniel Pratt to Barrington S. King, December 15, 1864, transcribed by Evelyn or Katherine Simpson. Mill No. 2 Employee List, May 1890 through December 1893, abstracted from original ledger in possession of Mr. Henry McGahee of Roswell.

Russell, Judge Lewis C. "Sweetwater History," *The Atlanta Journal,* 28 April 1932.

Rutherford, Mike. Interview by author. Old Perry County Courthouse Museum, Cannelton, Indiana. 8 May 1997.

Sapp, Shirley. Telephone conversation with author. Indianapolis, Indiana. 8 May 1997.

Schank, Margaret. Telephone conversation with author. Cannelton, Indiana. 7 May 1997.

"Sketch of the Life of Mrs. E. D. Boyd," *The Comanche* (Texas), October 1951.

Skinner, Arthur N. and James L., eds. *The Death of a Confederate.* Athens, Ga.: The University of Georgia Press, 1996.

Skinner, James L., ed. *The Autobiography of Henry Merrell: Industrial Missionary to the South.* Athens, Ga.: University of Georgia Press, 1991.

_____ Telephone conversation with author. Presbyterian College, Clinton, South Carolina. April and May 1997.

"Soldiers' Letters—Movements of the 4th Army Corps," *Cincinnati* (Ohio) *Daily Commercial,* 22 July 1864.

"Soldiers' Letters—Roswell Factory, Fording the Chattahoochee, and Marietta," *Cincinnati* (Ohio) *Daily Commercial,* 20 July 1864.

Steadman, E. *The Southern Manufacturer: Showing the Advantages of Manufacturing the Cotton in the Fields Where It Is Grown.* Gallatin, Tennessee: Gray & Boyers, 1858.

Sweetwater Creek State Park, Douglasville, Georgia. Letter from A. J. White to Margaret White, June 13, 1862. Park brochures.

Tell City Public Library, Tell City, Indiana. Genealogical holdings.

Factory Employees, Campbell County, Georgia, Militia Rolls, December 1863, abstracted by Joe Baggett, Douglasville, Georgia, April 1982.

New Manchester Village (Sweet Water Cotton Mill), 1860 census, abstracted by Verona Robertson Mitchem.

Roswell Millhand List abstracted from the 1860 census by George Kendley.

Temple, Sarah Blackwell Gober. *The First Hundred Years: A Short History of Cobb County, in Georgia.* Atlanta: Walter W. Brown Publishing Company, 1935.

Terrell, William H. H. and the Indiana Adjutant General's Office. *Indiana in the War of the Rebellion: Report of the Adjutant General.* Indiana Historical Bureau, 1960.

"A Terrible Storm," *Cincinnati* (Ohio) *Daily Commercial,* 25 July 1864.

Times (Evansville, Indiana), July 1864.

"To Be Sent North of the Ohio," *Louisville* (Kentucky) *Daily Journal,* 17 August 1864.

"Town Affairs," *Cannelton* (Indiana) *Reporter,* 13 September 1865.

Upson, Theodore Frelinghuysen. *With Sherman to the Sea: The Civil War Letters, Diaries & Reminiscences of Theodore F. Upson.* Baton Rouge, La.: Louisiana State University Press, 1943.

Wahl, Gloria. Interviews by author. Cannelton, Indiana. 1 April 1997 and 6-7 May 1997.

Walsh, Darlene M., ed. *Natalie Heath Merrill's Narrative History of Roswell, Georgia.* Roswell, Ga.: Walsh House, 1996.

Wanted notice in the classifieds section, *Cincinnati* (Ohio) *Daily Commercial,* 30 July 1864.

The War of the Rebellion: A Compilation of the Official Records of the Union and Confederate Armies. Harrisburg, Pa.: National Historical Society, 1971.

"War Reports," *Louisville* (Kentucky) *Anzeiger,* 19 July 1864.

"War Reports," *Louisville* (Kentucky) *Daily Evening News,* 24 July 1864.

Warner, Ezra J. *Generals in Blue: Lives of the Union Commanders.* Baton Rouge, La.: Louisiana State University Press, 1964.

_____. *Generals in Gray: Lives of the Confederate Commanders.* Baton Rouge, La.: Louisiana State University Press, 1959.

Warren, Mary Bondurant. *Alphabetical Index to Georgia's 1832 Gold Lottery.* Danielsville, Ga.: Heritage Papers, 1981.

Wiley, Bell I. *The Common Soldier of the Civil War.* New York: Charles Scribner's Sons, 1975.

_____. *The Plain People of the Confederacy.* Baton Rouge, La.: Louisiana State University Press, 1943.

Williams, David. *The Georgia Gold Rush: Twenty-Niners, Cherokees, and Gold Fever.* Columbia, S.C.: University of South Carolina Press, 1993.

Wills, Charles Wright. *Army Life of an Illinois Soldier, Including a Day by Day Record of Sherman's March to the Sea.* Washington, D.C.: Globe Printing Company, 1906

Winpenny, Thomas R. "Perils in Transferring Technology to the Frontier: A Case Study." *Journal of the Early Republic* 5, no. 4 (Winter 1985).

Winslow, Hattie Lou and Joseph R. H. Moore. *Camp Morton, 1861-1865, Indianapolis Prison Camp.* Indianapolis: Indiana Historical Society, 1940.

Wriston, Barbara. "Who Was the Architect of the Indiana Cotton Mill, 1849-1850?" *Journal of the Society of Archival Historians* 24, no. 2 (May 1965).

INDEX